The Bold Move cuts through the noise. It doesn't just talk about confidence, it shows you how to build it, and how to turn hesitation into momentum. The combination of honest stories and practical tools makes it refreshingly actionable; with Georgie's ambitious yet caring tone cutting across, it creates the perfect space to dream bigger and move forward. I genuinely wish I had read this 20 years ago, and look forward to using it now!

—**Eglantine Etiemble,** CTO, Pexa

The Bold Move is a masterclass in building confidence, leveraging your unique skills, and taking action before you feel ready. In a world where change is the only constant, Georgie's book is the essential guide we all need. Her insights are a powerful antidote to analysis paralysis, offering a clear, actionable roadmap for anyone looking to not just survive but thrive in the age of AI. If you're a professional wondering how to future-proof your career and lead, this book is your answer.

—**Marta James,** Chief Technology and
Product Officer, Humbli

A must-read for anyone grappling with imposter thoughts! Practical insights and strategies to help you reconnect with your WHY, Georgie brilliantly illustrates the power of action over waiting for confidence in your career and life.

—**Merryn Matthews,** Head of Technical Delivery,
7-Eleven Australia

Georgie has turned boldness into a lifestyle. Her career is a series of 'why not?' moments that show the rest of us what's possible when you dare to lead.

—**Francesca Salvo,** Industry Solutions Director & Victorian Branch Leader, Microsoft

This book is a revelation. In a world saturated with career advice that plays it safe, Georgie dares to ask — what if the real opportunity lies in being bold? It doesn't just identify a gap in the market; it fills it with courage, clarity and conviction. Every page is a nudge, a challenge, and a cheer for those ready to stop waiting and start moving. If you've ever felt stuck, uncertain or underestimated, this book is your call to action. It gave me the confidence to take the next step — and the tools to make it count.

—**Marlo Symons,** Transformation Leader & Change Strategist

Georgie Hubbard is a leader who doesn't just talk about bold moves — she lives them. She's built a movement that empowers women (and all who cross her path) to rise, act and lead with purpose. If you're ready for change, this book will be your trusted guide — filled with practical advice, tried-and-tested strategies, and the wisdom of someone who has been walking the walk for years. *The Bold Move* isn't just a read; it's an investment in your next level.

—**Wendy Zveglic,** Futurist of Work & AI Transformation Strategist

THE
BOLD
MOVE

THE
BUILD CONFIDENCE &
BOLD
REINVENT YOUR CAREER
MOVE
IN THE AGE OF AI

GEORGIE HUBBARD

WILEY

First published 2026 by John Wiley & Sons Australia, Ltd

ISBN: 978-1-394-37778-7

A catalogue record for this book is available from the National Library of Australia

Registered Office
John Wiley & Sons Australia, Ltd. Level 4, 600 Bourke Street, Melbourne, VIC 3000, Australia

For details of our global editorial offices, customer services, and more information about Wiley products visit us at www.wiley.com.

Wiley also publishes its books in a variety of electronic formats and by print-on-demand. Some content that appears in standard print versions of this book may not be available in other formats.

Cover Design: Paul McCarthy
Cover image: © 4khz/Getty Images

Set in 11.5/16.5 pt and Warnock Pro, Straive, Chennai, India.
Printed and bound by CPI Group (UK) Ltd, Croydon, CR0 4YY
C9781394377787_121125
The manufacturer's authorized representative according to the EU General Product Safety Regulation is Wiley-VCH GmbH, Boschstr. 12, 69469 Weinheim, Germany, e-mail: Product_Safety@wiley.com.

CONTENTS

FOREWORD

History is the study of past events, especially those concerning human activity, societies and civilisations. In the 1970s, the term 'herstory' emerged during the second wave of feminism as both a serious rallying cry, aiming to compensate for the male-dominated nature of conventional history, and a way to bring attention to the lives, deeds and participation of women in shaping the future of humanity.

As we stand on the edge of an AI era, we are faced with an extraordinary challenge. How do we embrace algorithms augmenting the technology that is going to touch all facets of life when these algorithms are trained on data overwhelmingly entrenched in bias that excludes, diminishes and, in some cases, erases our herstory? Our wisdom, discoveries, inventions, trials and wars that broke through injustice, built communities and the very fabric of our society sit in the hands of an algorithm. A bunch of maths deployed into apps that download to our devices, a short cut to the future — or a fast path to exclusion.

The dot-com era in the 1990s and the tech boom of the 2010s fundamentally transformed the landscape of high-status careers, shifting the centre of financial and cultural power from traditional fields such as finance, law and medicine to technology. These waves of tech advancement gave rise to a new archetype: the 'tech bro'. This led to the under-representation of women and minorities in technical roles, which, in turn, has directly contributed to the embedding of bias in AI and other technologies.

I see this moment in our history as a call to action. For women and every person in a minority to step forward and take a seat at the AI table. Start that AI course. Join a women in tech community. Subscribe to that AI podcast. The ability to see the future and make a decision to learn towards it is often not offered to everyone but those in the know.

This book is your call to action. Georgie is shouting from the rooftops that it's time make a move — a bold move.

Extraordinary power comes from making a bold move; one courageous decision can redefine the entire trajectory of your career. Stepping forward to seize this moment, learn AI skills or take a career audit is not just an act of personal ambition, but also a statement of possibility for everyone who follows.

Each bold step you take opens doors for your own growth, and helps break barriers and inspire others to dream bigger. Remember — the hardest journeys often begin with a single, courageous step. If you are reading this, you are already on your way. Trust your talent, embrace your potential and let your boldness shape the future you deserve.

KB (Katherine Boiciuc)
Chief Technology Officer Oceania, EY

ABOUT THE AUTHOR

Georgie Hubbard has spent over a decade shaping the future of careers. With 12 years in technology recruitment, Georgie has interviewed and placed thousands of professionals across Australia, giving her a unique insight into what gets someone hired and the skills that companies are really looking for.

As one of the directors of CH Solutions, a technology recruitment firm she built from the ground up, Georgie has become a trusted adviser to both individuals and global organisations navigating change, growth and reinvention.

A true expert at the intersection of recruitment, career development and personal growth, her insights are grounded in real-world hiring experience, making her uniquely equipped to guide women through career pivots, confidence-building and the pursuit of meaningful work, especially in today's rapidly evolving tech landscape.

With a passion for building inclusive workplaces and a clear-eyed view of the gender gap in tech, three years ago Georgie launched Sisterhood Club, an initiative designed to elevate, empower and expand the role of women in technology and AI. Through sell-out events, a mentorship program connecting emerging professionals with senior leaders and over 150 episodes of the Career Confidence podcast, she's helped hundreds of women believe in themselves, step into their potential and own their place in the future of work.

In addition to her work through the Sisterhood Club, Georgie has delivered Career Confidence workshops and coaching programs inside some of Australia's leading companies. Her sessions go beyond theory, equipping professionals with tangible tools to build self-belief, elevate their visibility and develop the executive presence needed to lead in today's workplace. With her signature mix of practicality and inspiration, Georgie empowers individuals to step into their next chapter with clarity and conviction.

At the heart of Georgie's work is a deep belief that the future of work must be inclusive, equitable and accessible to all. Her mission is to ensure that as industries evolve, especially in tech and AI, no-one is left behind. Whether she's mentoring an emerging leader, advising a hiring manager or speaking on stage, Georgie is driven by a singular vision: to create a world where everyone, regardless of background or identity, feels confident stepping into their career potential.

INTRODUCTION
THE CONFIDENCE GAP IS HOLDING YOU BACK

I was standing at the front of a boardroom, leading a career development workshop for one of Australia's most respected financial services organisations. The room was packed with women of all ages, from mid-level managers to rising executives, all eager to learn how to take the next step in their careers.

Alongside my recruitment company, CH Solutions, I have been running these workshops for a couple of years, coaching professionals on how to get ahead in their careers, and improve their leadership skills and confidence. But that day, I decided to try something new.

I asked the group, 'On a scale from 1 to 10, how confident do you feel in your ability to step up in your career?'

Silence.

The women glanced at each other, hesitant, as if waiting for someone else to go first. Then, slowly, they began writing their numbers down.

'Who put themselves at a ten?' I asked.

No hands.

'An eight?' A few hands were raised. 'A seven?' Five hands went up, just five. 'A six?' More hands this time but, still, a lot of the women in the room hadn't moved. 'A five?' More hands. Then I asked, 'Who put themselves at a four or below?'

One by one, the remaining hands rose. My heart sank. This wasn't a room full of entry-level professionals. These were smart, capable women, some with years of experience, huge leadership potential and glowing recommendations. On paper, they had everything they needed to take the next step. But in their minds, they were stuck.

So I then asked the group if anyone would be open to sharing why they chose the number they did.

A few women nodded. Then, one by one, they spoke. Here's some of what they shared:

- 'I second-guess myself all the time. I feel like an impostor.'

- 'I just came back from parental leave, and I feel shaky, like I've lost my voice in decision making.'

- 'I have ideas that could solve real problems in my department, but in meetings, I can't seem to find the words to speak up.'

- 'I'm working in a male-dominated team, and I often feel overlooked and that my voice or opinions don't seem to matter. It makes me really question my ability.'

Their words hit me hard.

These weren't issues of skill or capability but of confidence. These women weren't held back by a lack of knowledge or talent. They were holding themselves back.

This was the moment I realised something profound: we don't have a skill gap; we have a confidence gap.

The truth about success

I've been in the recruitment industry for over 12 years and launched my own agency, CH Solutions, seven years ago (more on that wild ride to come). Over the course of my career, I've interviewed thousands of candidates, placed hundreds of professionals in top roles, and coached multiple businesses on how to hire and retain the best talent. I've seen firsthand what separates those who land the job, get the promotion and rise into leadership, and those who don't — and it's not always talent, experience or hard skills.

Here's what it often comes down to:

- It's having confidence and the belief in your ability to figure things out before you feel ready.

- It's applying for a job even though you meet only 60 per cent of the qualifications.

- It's negotiating your salary without hesitation.

- It's pitching yourself unapologetically.

Confidence isn't just a 'nice-to-have' trait. It's the deciding factor in who succeeds and who stays stuck.

Yet, through my workshops, recruitment interviews and panels at major events, I've learned that most people, especially women, don't believe they have it. They downplay their accomplishments, hesitate to speak up in meetings and second-guess their worth. As a result, they remain in roles they've outgrown, underpaid and overworked, fading into the background while watching others move ahead.

That stops now.

Why I wrote this book

I wrote this book because I've been there myself. I know what it feels like to question whether you're ready to take the next step. I know what it's like to doubt whether you belong in the room, at the table or on the stage. But I also know what happens when you learn to trust yourself, take bold action and stop waiting for permission.

Over the years, I've helped thousands of professionals break through self-doubt and build the confidence to:

- change careers — even when they thought it was too late

- negotiate a salary increase — even when they feared rejection

- step into leadership — even when they didn't feel 100 per cent ready.

This book isn't about waiting to feel more confident. It's about learning how to take action despite self-doubt, and building real, lasting career confidence in the process.

You don't need another degree. You don't need another year of experience. You don't need permission.

You just need to start. You need to make your bold move.

And this book will show you how.

What to expect from this book

This isn't just another career book filled with generic advice.

For years, I've been on a mission to understand why some professionals achieve extraordinary success while others, equally talented, struggle to move forward. What makes the difference?

Through thousands of interviews, coaching sessions and real-world observations, I've uncovered a powerful truth: success isn't random. It follows patterns, specific behaviours, choices and actions that, when adopted, can transform careers and lives. And the best part is that these patterns aren't reserved for a select few. They're learnable.

Over the last decade, I've sat across from thousands of professionals as a recruiter, helping them navigate career transitions and land leadership roles. I've co-founded Sisterhood Club, a community designed to elevate women in tech, and launched a mentorship program connecting ambitious women with Australia's top executives. I've led career workshops for global companies, giving professionals the tools to step up, speak out and take control of their futures.

And through hosting the Career Confidence podcast, I've had the privilege of interviewing hundreds of CEOs, entrepreneurs and industry leaders, uncovering exactly what separates those who thrive from those who merely survive.

This book brings it all together — the lessons, the strategies and the real-world success patterns — so you can apply them to your own career and unlock the confidence and courage to go after what you truly want.

Throughout this book, I share:

- real stories and lessons from top leaders, entrepreneurs and professionals who have navigated career transitions, overcome setbacks and built unshakable confidence

- proven strategies to help you step into leadership, negotiate your worth and take bold career moves, even when you don't feel ready

- practical exercises designed to master your mindset, develop career resilience and take action

- the future skills needed, both hard and human, that will ensure you stay ahead in this new world of work

- strategies to help you stand out in a competitive marketplace by building your personal brand.

So grab your journal, notebook or preferred device for making notes, and get ready to work your way through these exercises and reflections as you read.

Then, at the end of the book, I share my 30-Day Bold Move Challenge — a formula to help you transition, through daily practical strategies, from where you are now to where the future career opportunities will be.

The workplace is changing faster than ever. AI, automation and rapid technological advancements are reshaping industries, making adaptability one of the most important skills of all. The way we work, the roles we hold and the skills we need are evolving, but confidence remains the constant that determines success.

This book is your guide to navigating these changes with certainty, making bold career moves in an uncertain world, and ensuring that no matter what shifts around you, you remain in control of your future.

My goal is for you to walk away with a step-by-step guide to building confidence, breaking through self-doubt and unlocking your full potential, no matter what stage of your career you're in.

So are you ready to stop playing small, take action, develop unwavering confidence and future-proof your career? Then let's dive in.

PART I

MINDSET SHIFTS TO HELP YOU BUILD UNSHAKABLE CONFIDENCE

What you need to believe before you can achieve career success.

Chapter 1

Understanding courage, not confidence, drives success

I n this chapter, I break down the confidence myth and get honest about what it really takes to build confidence that lasts. I look at how fear keeps us small, why waiting to 'feel ready' is a trap, and what it means to move forward anyway. I also outline the three Cs that quietly steal your confidence, as well as the three Cs that will help you rebuild it. And I share the personal moments where I backed myself before I felt fully prepared.

By the end, you won't just understand confidence — you'll have the tools to take your next bold move, even if fear is still sitting beside you.

The 'Aha!' moment

I used to believe that confident people were just born that way — that they had something I didn't, some innate, unshakable self-belief that made them walk into rooms with ease, speak up without hesitation and go after opportunities without second-guessing themselves. I thought confidence was the prerequisite for success. You build confidence first, and then you take action.

But after years of working with top professionals, coaching hundreds of job seekers and interviewing some incredibly successful people, I've learned something that changed everything for me: confidence doesn't come first; courage does.

Think about the moments in your life when you felt the most confident. Maybe it was after you nailed a big presentation, landed a job offer or spoke out in public. Did you feel confident before you did it, or did confidence come after you proved to yourself that you could?

Having to feel ready before you start is one of the biggest myths about confidence. The truth is you'll likely never feel ready, and if you wait for confidence before taking action, you'll stay exactly where you are — and this is where fear comes into the equation.

Every career professional I have met has fears:

- fear of failure

- fear of not being good enough

- fear of what others will think of us

- fear of success.

The list goes on. Most of us believe fear is a red flag, a warning sign that we're heading into dangerous territory. But when it comes to personal and professional growth, I have come to realise that fear isn't a stop sign; it's a signal that you're stretching beyond your comfort zone.

Think about the moments in your life when you've felt the most nervous or uncertain. Were those also the moments when you grew the most?

For me, they definitely were. Growth has never come when everything felt easy. I have grown the most when faced with challenges. When pushing myself to do the thing that scared me, and going beyond my comfort zone. The first time we try anything new, we have to be prepared to suck a little. We can prepare, practise and do everything we can to try to control the outcome, but when we start something new, our performance is never going to be flawless — and that's okay!

If we spend our lives and careers avoiding anything new out of fear — whether that's fear of failure, judgement or the unknown — we risk staying stuck. Playing it safe only leads to one outcome — waking up one day and wondering, 'How did I get here?' For me, regret has become the scariest possibility of all. I don't want to reach the end of my long, precious life and think, *If only*. That thought terrifies me far more than contemplating a few bold risks, feeling the fear, and doing it anyway.

One book that deeply moved me was Bronnie Ware's *The Top Five Regrets of the Dying*. As a palliative care nurse, Ware sat with people at the end of their lives and listened as they shared their regrets. These regrets weren't about things they did — they were about what they didn't do. The missed chances, the dreams unpursued and the lives unlived.

The number one regret Ware uncovered was, 'I wish I'd had the courage to live a life true to myself, not the life others expected of me'.

So next time you hesitate, worried about what people might think, afraid you'll fail, questioning whether you're good enough, remember this: at the end of your life, it won't be the failures that haunt you. It'll be the dreams, the goals and the outcomes you were too scared to pursue.

Fear often appears not because we're incapable but because we're stepping into something new. It's a natural response when we're pushing our limits and doing something that matters. Your brain isn't telling you to stop; it's just registering unfamiliarity.

Threat perception and your brain

Imagine this for a second: you're standing on the edge of a high diving board, contemplating leaping to the water far below. You've never dived from such a height, and your palms are beginning to sweat. Your heart races and your stomach tightens.

You know logically that it's safe. People have jumped before you and no harm has come to them, but your body doesn't care about such logic. Your brain has evolved to prioritise safety over opportunity. It sees the unknown as a risk, even when it's not. This is why activities such as public speaking, career transitions and stepping into leadership roles trigger fear.

But here's something important to remember: fear and excitement feel the same in the body. Your heart races, your breathing quickens and your body floods with adrenaline. The only difference is the story you attach to it — and understanding this is something that has made a huge difference in my life.

Try reframing fear from 'I'm not ready' to 'I'm growing', or 'I'm nervous' to 'I'm excited'. This simple reframe has been a saving grace in my career, and I use it whenever I step up and do something that feels new and uncomfortable. Early in my career, one of those moments of stepping up was deciding to get better at public speaking. Here's how I reframed and overcame my fear.

Boldly choosing courage over fear

The fear of public speaking, known as glossophobia, is one of the most common fears among individuals worldwide. Experts estimate around 75 per cent of the population experiences some degree of anxiety when it comes to speaking in public, and I am certainly one of them! In the early years of my career, I couldn't even stand up in front of my colleagues and say my name without almost passing out. My heart would race and sweat would pour every time I had to present. I knew this would hold me back in my career so I took action and enrolled in Toastmasters, an organisation where you can practise public speaking, and gain constructive feedback.

I can honestly say I almost talked myself out of going every week. It was massively outside of my comfort zone, but I knew I had to keep showing up and doing the work, because that was how I was going to begin overcoming my fear — not by running from it, but by facing it head on.

The beautiful thing was that everyone there was so supportive, and I began having more of an active role,

(continued)

which slowly but surely built my confidence. After a number of weeks, it was my turn to deliver a five-minute speech. I remember practising in front of the mirror and recording myself over and over again, until the day arrived when I had to stand up in front of the room and deliver it. To say I was nervous would be a massive understatement, but despite the nerves, a few scrambled words and plenty of 'ums', I did it. I can't tell you how good I felt afterwards. Over the course of a year, I rarely missed a week and, over time, as I was able to calm myself and reframe those nervous butterflies into excitement, my public speaking began to improve.

A couple of years later, I had to take what I had practised in the safety of the Toastmasters classroom and apply it to a real-world speaking engagement.

I still remember the moment I was about to step out in front of a large audience. I had been invited to present at a career expo, an event filled with accomplished professionals and industry leaders. I was there to speak about accelerating career growth, something I had spent years advising clients on. But as I stood at the side of the stage, waiting for my turn, I felt like I was back at the beginning again as my mind started racing.

'Who am I to be up here?'

'What if I fall flat on my face?'

'What if I forget what I'm supposed to say?'

'What if they think I don't belong?'

The self-doubt was loud. My hands were clammy, my heart pounded in my chest and, for a split second, I considered backing out. But then I caught myself. I said, 'Georgie you've got this. This is what you have been training for'.

I reminded myself that if I waited to feel confident before stepping onto that stage, I would never do it. First, I must have courage.

I took a deep breath, walked onto that stage and started speaking. And you know what? It wasn't perfect. My voice shook at first and my mouth was so dry, but as I kept going, the nerves settled. The preparation and all the Toastmaster sessions started to pay off. The more I spoke, the more confident I became. By the time I finished, I was energised and excited. Most importantly, I had proven to myself that I could stand in front of an audience and deliver a speech.

For the next 24 hours, I let myself ride the high, feeling proud that I'd had the courage to step outside my comfort zone. I hoped that what I had shared had resonated with those who had listened to my presentation.

Once the adrenaline had settled, I sat down with my journal, took a breath, and reflected. First, I acknowledged what I had done well. I let myself fully feel that sense of accomplishment, resisting the urge to brush past it too quickly.

Then, I asked myself what I could have done differently. What would have made this presentation even better?

Notice the language here. In the early days of Toastmasters, I used to ask, 'What did I do wrong?' And, before I knew it, my brain had gone into overdrive, searching for all the ways I had fallen short. Every fumble, every missed point, every tiny mistake would suddenly feel magnified.

But I learned to shift my questioning to, 'What would have made this even better?' and with that shift my mindset also changed. Instead of dwelling on failures, I started looking for ways to improve. I wasn't tearing myself down, I was building myself up.

Over the years, I've learned that confidence isn't just about taking action; it's also about training your mind to focus on possibilities rather than limitations. The words you use internally shape the beliefs you carry externally, and those beliefs dictate the actions you choose.

If I hadn't taken that first courageous step and enrolled in Toastmasters, I would never have delivered that speech or had the confidence to say yes to any of the speaking opportunities that followed. That one decision didn't just help me speak in front of a room; it helped me see myself differently.

So don't wait until you feel ready; instead, show up, even with the nerves, and prove to yourself that you can do things that bring on fear. Every time I've stretched beyond what felt comfortable, I've grown, and that's what I want you to remember. It's not about being fearless, it's about being willing — willing to back yourself, even when you're unsure. Your growth and opportunities live just on the other side of the bold moves you're brave enough to make.

So the next time fear shows up, don't see it as a reason to back down. See it as a signal that you're exactly where you need to be.

The pros and cons of faking it till you make it

The phrase 'fake it till you make it' is thrown around a lot when it comes to confidence and overcoming fear or impostor syndrome. The idea is simple: act as if you already have the confidence, and eventually the act will become real. It's a strategy that has helped many professionals push through self-doubt.

But does it actually work?

The pros: Why 'faking it' can help you grow

I've had the privilege of interviewing some top C-suite executives on the Career Confidence podcast, and many of my guests have shared how stepping into roles before they felt ready was the key to unlocking new career opportunities. One standout conversation from the podcast that showcases this in action was with Lauren, a senior executive at a large financial institution.

Lauren's story: Acting boldly before you feel ready

Lauren, an executive leader at a large financial company, never waited until she felt 100 per cent ready before taking her next step. In fact, she describes most of her bold career moves as moments when she was about 50 per cent sure she could do the job. In those moments, she decided she could figure out the other 50 per cent along the way.

Her journey started in recruitment before she transitioned into change management, a field she had been recruiting for but had never actually worked in. Instead of sitting on the sidelines, she saw an opportunity, walked into the client's office and pitched herself for the role, despite having no formal experience in it.

That moment set the tone for the rest of her career. Time and again, she stepped into leadership roles without feeling fully prepared. She learned that growth happens in what she calls the stretch zone, where discomfort forces you to level up.

One of the biggest shifts in Lauren's leadership journey was realising that perfection isn't the goal—progress is. She had to let go of the need to have all the answers, and

(continued)

embrace the fact that learning and leadership go hand in hand. She surrounded herself with the right people, built a strong team and developed confidence through experience, not before it.

This is where the idea of 'fake it till you make it' comes into play.

Lauren admitted that she didn't feel qualified when she first stepped into a leadership role. But instead of waiting to feel ready, she acted as if she belonged, showing up with confidence, speaking up in meetings and making decisions decisively. Over time, those actions built real confidence.

You might think confidence comes from feeling ready. But research shows the opposite is to be true. When you act confident — speaking clearly, holding eye contact and standing tall — your brain begins to believe it. This is the core of self-perception theory, a psychological principle introduced by Daryl Bem, which suggests that we learn about who we are by watching what we do.

So, in this sense, 'faking it' can work. It helps you push through discomfort, take opportunities you might otherwise shy away from and build competence through experience.

However, like anything in life, there is always an opposing force.

The cons: The risk of feeling like a fraud

If 'faking it' isn't backed by action and growth, it can lead to impostor syndrome. Pretending to be confident without actually developing the skills or doing the work can make you feel even more like a fraud. I've seen this throughout my recruitment career, with candidates who project confidence but crumble when asked deeper questions about their skills and experience.

So 'fake it till you make it' isn't enough. Instead, act before you feel ready, but then do the work. Don't wait for confidence to arrive before you take action, and make sure every step forward is backed by effort and learning. If you want to be a leader, start leading in small ways. If you want to be a great public speaker, put yourself in situations where you can practise. Doing so means you're not faking it; you're stepping into it, doing the work and allowing confidence to follow.

So, yes, act before you feel ready. But don't fake — face, do and become it.

Understanding the confidence equation

I am always looking and listening for patterns. I am innately curious by nature, and throughout my recruitment career, I have tried to figure out what drives people's career success.

I have put it down to a few factors, but all of them tie back into confidence. If you don't believe you are capable of achieving something, you won't even take the first step towards it. Knowing this, I have identified three behaviours people do that squander confidence, and three behaviours people work on to boost it.

Let's break these down.

The 3Cs that steal confidence

The three behaviours I see that reduce or steal confidence are complaining, criticising and comparing. Here's how these destructive '3Cs' work against you.

Complaining

I am sure you know someone in your life who is always moaning, blaming and playing the victim. They seem to go from one problem to the next. It's like chaos follows them. They are quick to tell you why they can't do something or why life is unfair. Nothing is ever their fault — it's because of the boss, the co-worker, the government or economy, their parents, siblings, children, spouse, you get the idea. This victim mindset steals confidence and becomes a self-fulfilling prophecy.

We've all been there, or maybe you're in this spiral right now. If you are, don't worry — by the end of this book, by working through all the activities, you won't be.

Blaming and complaining are two of the quickest ways to steal your power and chip away at your self-belief. At one point in my life, I was quick to blame anyone or anything but myself. It gave me the excuse not to act and, for a while, made me feel less inadequate in front of my peers. However, it also made me doubt my abilities and play small, which is not an empowering place to be. I decided something had to change. I made the conscious choice to take radical responsibility for everything in my life.

However, instead of jumping into judgement and being critical (see the next section for more on this), I focused on what was in my power to influence, and the areas of my life I wanted to focus on improving first.

I decided to start with my business, which I had neglected. I had stepped back from the important day-to-day tasks and, as a result, CH Solutions was beginning to struggle. Since this was my main income stream, I knew I needed to stop blaming the economy, the team and the clients (and whoever else I could think of) and do one thing daily that would move the needle in the right direction. I made a list of ideas and picked five things I could execute on that week.

I knew if I delayed, things would get worse, and I could talk myself out of not acting. As a result of this exercise, I immediately felt a sense of drive and determination, and I began to make progress, which built momentum. The moment I stopped complaining and blaming was the moment I felt empowered to take back control, have courage and to begin building confidence in myself again. I encourage you to catch yourself anytime you start complaining about something, especially if it is outside your control, and instead focus on the things that are in your power to influence. Start by looking at the areas that you have been neglecting. As you do this, ensure you don't jump into the next C ...

Criticising

I have a confession to make ... I used to be addicted to judgement and criticism. I would judge not only myself, but also others. In my late 20s, this judging and criticising was so automatic I wasn't even consciously aware of it. I would put myself down and focus on my weaknesses and all my shortcomings. If something went wrong at work, I was so quick to criticise. And then, to make myself feel better, I would put others down too. I wouldn't say it to their face, but I would think it, which sometimes is even worse.

My thoughts went like this: *God, Georgie you suck at recruitment. Maybe you should quit, leave Australia and move back to the United Kingdom. You just don't have what it takes. You will never be as good as [insert co-workers' names] at recruitment.* This would run through my mind daily. To make myself feel mildly more adequate, I would then look to someone else in the office and think, *Could be worse — you could be like [insert different co-worker's name]. They are useless, unorganised and couldn't even sell prosecco at a hen do.*

Overtime, I have realised that criticism and putting ourselves and others down is one of the quickest and most effective ways to erode our self-worth. I never used to feel good when I judged others and, even as I was doing it, I knew it was just shining a spotlight back on my own insecurities.

If you want to build confidence, you must become aware of your inner dialogue. I delve into this much more deeply in the next chapters, but for now just make a conscious effort to notice when your inner critic shows up. What does this critic say to you, and how does that make you feel about yourself?

I have noticed my inner critic talks the loudest when I am focusing on the next C ...

Comparing

We live in a world where a touch of a button, a swipe of a thumb and a flick of a finger can make us feel like we are the biggest failure and that we aren't where we 'should' be!

Welcome to the world of social media. Without giving away my age, I grew up in a time before mobile phones and the internet existed and, to be completely honest, I am so grateful I did. I am not here to diss social media or technology. However grateful I am that I grew up without it, I am equally grateful it now exists. I would not be able to run my business, grow my brand or do half of the things I do now without it.

The issue is this. Never in the history of humanity has it been so easy to compare ourselves to complete strangers. As if it wasn't enough to peek over the garden fence and attempt to keep up with the Jones's perfectly striped lawn next door, now we are trying to keep up with the rest of the world. It's no wonder anxiety and depression are on the rise!

Whether you love it or hate it, social media and technology are here to stay, and we can choose to use it or be used by it. I found myself in my personal version of doomscrolling a few months back. I started by clicking through my friend's recent photos, capturing what looked like an amazing holiday to Bali. Then I clicked on another person's profile and found out they had just brought their dream home. Then I decided to really make myself feel like a total loser and spiral further, clicking on profiles for people I had never even met. And, oh boy — did I soon really feel like I wasn't good enough, pretty enough, smart enough, rich enough, healthy enough and happy enough!

And social media isn't the only place where comparison kicks in. It can also happen within your workplace, family and friendship group. I know what it's like to compare yourself and put yourself down in the process, but it only leads down one path — self-doubt.

However, a healthier way to live life is possible that can turn comparison into your superpower. I know because I have reframed this in my own life to boost my confidence, not erode it.

The next time you see or hear that someone you know has achieved something you would like to achieve, whether it's a promotion, a new home, improved their health or something else you admire, use that. This is direct feedback, teaching you something about yourself. How you respond next is the crucial part. If you come up with a list of excuses as to why you could never achieve what they have, stop yourself. Remember — this is one of the least empowering things you can do. Instead, stop the inner critic and negative self-talk and think to yourself, *If they can do it, so can I!*

You don't have to have everything figured out or even know the next step; all you need to understand is that they have proven what is possible, and if you want whatever they have bad enough, you can always find a way.

In the following chapters, I help you define what success means to you, so you can stop chasing someone else's version. For now, know that, yes, comparison is the thief of joy; however, when used strategically, it can be a motivator for change.

Now you know the 3Cs that steal your confidence, take a moment and reflect on what C has shown up the most in your life so far — because once you are aware of something, you have the power to change it.

The 3Cs that build confidence

The 3Cs that build confidence are courage, competence and clarity. Let's explore just why these are so important.

Courage

I will repeat this message throughout the book because I believe it is incredibly important to remember: first comes courage, and then comes confidence.

Over my recruitment career, I have seen far too many talented individuals held back — not by their talent or skill, but by their lack of courage to step into the unknown. We are entering a decade of change, and those of us who choose to be bold and brave will enter a season of opportunity and prosperity. Having courage is no longer an option; it's an essential.

When I look back at my life thus far, I can pinpoint moments where I decided to choose faith over fear, and courage over comfort — and I have never regretted these decisions.

My first bold move — to the other side of the world

At 23, I packed a rucksack, left my home in the United Kingdom, kissed my parents goodbye, and flew to Australia to start my new life. Did I feel ready or confident? Absolutely not, but I knew I would regret not giving life in Australia a go.

I still remember landing in Melbourne Airport. Being British and growing up watching *Home and Away*, I thought Australia was always warm. But that day, getting off the plane and waiting to catch a Skybus into the city to take me to the hostel, I realised that *no*, Australia could, in fact, be freezing! Digging around in my rucksack, I pulled out my only jumper and quickly put it on.

I remember arriving at the hostel, tired after a 24-hour flight, and thinking, *God, it really is the other side of the world.* I felt a wave of emotion thinking about my family, whom I had waved goodbye to not so long ago. Stepping into the hostel made it even worse. Online, it had looked clean, modern and full of what looked like happy backpackers living the Aussie dream. Unfortunately, that was not the reality. I walked into a funky-smelling, messy reception

(continued)

area and was greeted by a woman who looked like she hadn't smiled or seen sunlight in years. I said my name and attempted to strike up a conversation, but was curtly told my room wasn't ready and I couldn't check in until 3 pm (it was only 10 am). I asked if I could have a shower, but was told they were all being cleaned so I would have to come back in an hour. After a long-haul flight, all you want to do is have a shower and catch a breath. Still hopeful for a tiny amount of help, I asked if there was anywhere to leave my rucksack. Her response: no space to store it.

I could feel myself getting more and more emotional, so I thanked her, said I'd see her in an hour and went off to find a café to sit in.

Sitting down in one of the cool little alleyways in Melbourne with a cup of coffee, I remember thinking to myself, *You've got this. Be brave.*

When I look back on this moment in my life, I am filled with pure love for younger Georgie. The following weeks and months were some of the loneliest, emotionally charged, but also most empowering times of my life. Not a day went by when I wasn't on Skyscanner looking at flights back to the United Kingdom or Facetiming my family, close to tears. Throughout this period, I knew I had to give it just one more day. I soon found a flat to share with some lovely girls who had also just arrived in Melbourne, and got a job running a local skin clinic. (More on my career pivot into tech recruitment to come.)

That one more day turned into one more week, one more month and then one more year. Now, 12 years later, I am an Australian citizen, have some amazing friends, a wonderful husband, the cutest dog called Ted and my own business, and I am proud to call this country my home.

I hope my story shows that when you show up with courage and back yourself, whatever stage of life you are at, you will be met with both the good and the bad, the challenge and the opportunity. This is what growth looks like. It's not a safe and comfortable path, but it's where all the momentum begins. When it gets hard, we need to have the courage to take one small step or one day at a time.

When it comes to your career, courage can look like putting your hand up to pitch an idea, offering your thoughts or feedback in a meeting, learning a new skill, seeking out a mentor, attending a networking event. It's these moments when you choose to back yourself that will result in you building the next C and dramatically boost your confidence ...

Competence

In order to excel in your career and build confidence, you must continue to invest in your personal growth. Having the courage to begin is the first step, but it must be backed up by action and skill acquisition. As covered earlier in this chapter, faking it till you make it will get you in the right room but without the required substance it won't get you a seat at the table.

I dive into the skills you need to future-proof your career in the chapters to come, so I won't go into the details here. What I want you to remember right now is that hiring managers consistently ask for candidates with two types of skills: hard skills and soft skills — or what I like to call human skills. Both will be equally important as we continue to move through this next decade.

Deciding what skills you will focus on the most is where the next C comes into play ...

Clarity

In a world full of distractions and noise, the more you stay anchored to your own values, ambitions and goals, the more confident and successful you will be. Without clarity, confidence will be fleeting, because you will always second-guess yourself whenever you begin to think about something new.

When you know what you want, why you want it, and who you need to become to achieve it, confidence will show up as you take the right steps to get there.

Without clarity, you may find yourself drifting from one thing to the next without a plan for getting there. By the end of this book, if you work through the exercises and implement the strategies provided, you will know exactly what you want and why, and have a step-by-step guide to achieving the outcome you deserve.

For now, start thinking about what you like and dislike about your current position. This will set the groundwork for the chapters ahead.

A small, bold step to get started

In this first chapter, I've stressed that confidence comes from taking action before you feel ready. So now it's time to take a small, but bold step. You don't always need to make a huge leap; small, consistent actions are often the key to creating long-lasting change.

Identify one small thing you can do in the next 24 hours that pushes you outside your comfort zone. This should be something simple but slightly uncomfortable — just enough to create a stretch.

Here are some ideas:

- Speak up in a meeting when you'd usually stay quiet.

- Send a LinkedIn message to someone you admire.

- Ask a question in a group setting, even if it makes you nervous.

- Share an idea at work that you've been holding back.

- Start a conversation with someone new.

And here's how to put it into action:

1. *Pick one action that feels like a slight stretch:* Write it down on your notepad, device or journal.

2. *Do it within 24 hours:* No overthinking, just act.

3. *Afterwards, take one minute to reflect:* How did that feel? What did you learn?

Remember—the goal isn't perfection but progress. By taking this small step, you're proving to yourself that you can act before you feel ready.

The more you repeat this, the more confident you will become. Because confidence isn't a switch you flip; it's a muscle you build.

Chapter 2

Overcoming impostor syndrome and self-doubt

In this chapter, I dive into something that's followed me at every stage of my career: impostor syndrome. I explore exactly what it is, how it shows up and why it can have such a grip on high achievers, especially when we're on the edge of growth.

More importantly, I show you how to stop it from talking you out of your next bold move. I walk you through three practical steps to quiet the inner critic, and provide three powerful questions that will help you build momentum, make clear decisions and move forward with confidence.

Self-doubt is a sign of growth

I only started to understand what impostor syndrome actually meant a few years ago, even though I had experienced a number of the symptoms correlated with it. So, what even is it? According to Oxford Languages, impostor syndrome is, 'The persistent inability to believe that one's success is deserved or has been legitimately achieved as a result of one's own efforts or skills'.

People who experience impostor syndrome often believe they are a 'fraud' and fear being exposed, even though they've earned their achievements through hard work and skill. They tie their success to luck, timing or other external factors rather than their own ability, and often feel they are not really deserving of the success they have accomplished.

Some signs of impostor syndrome can include:

- doubting your achievements

- feeling like you're 'faking it'

- attributing success to external factors ('I was just lucky')

- fearing being 'found out' or exposed as not good enough

- overworking to 'prove' your worth

- avoiding new opportunities for fear of failure

- constantly comparing yourself to others

- feeling like you need to gain another qualification because you're 'not ready yet'.

Looking at this list, I can clearly see how impostor syndrome has affected my career. Overworking, doubting my achievements and comparing myself to others have all been constants throughout my life. However, by adopting certain habits and equipping myself with certain tools, I no longer allow impostor syndrome to take hold and prevent me from bold moves and stepping up into my true potential.

Something I have noticed when dealing with my own impostor syndrome is that it often shows up at the exact moment I'm pushing myself to do something new. It often surfaces not when I'm comfortable, but when I'm expanding, stepping into a new role, stretching my skill set or sitting in rooms I had once only dreamed of being in. I've realised it's my brain's slightly clumsy way of protecting me from risk and trying to keep me safe. But it's really signalling that I'm on the edge of something important: growth.

We don't talk about this enough. Impostor syndrome is not a flaw; it's feedback, and it doesn't come up when we are playing safe or remaining stagnant. It comes up when we are stepping into the unknown.

The other thing we don't often talk about is that not everyone experiences impostor syndrome. And if you don't, that doesn't make you arrogant, overconfident or unaware; it simply means self-doubt doesn't show up in the same way for you. Own that!

I recently saw an interview with American rugby union star Ilona Maher, in which she was asked whether she ever struggles with impostor syndrome. Her response? 'I don't have that!' No hesitation, no qualifying statements, just a confident smile and pure, unapologetic self-assurance. Go, Ilona!!

I loved everything about that moment. Not just because it was refreshing, but because it challenged a narrative we hear so often — that to be ambitious, to strive and to grow, we must feel like frauds along the way. Ilona reminded us that it's not a requirement.

Let's be clear, confidence isn't arrogance. It's not pretending. It's owning the work you've done, the hours you've invested and the talent you've cultivated, and being okay with knowing that you deserve to be exactly where you are. And that deserves to be celebrated.

So if you're reading this and thinking, *Actually, I don't really experience impostor syndrome*, amazing, own it. That doesn't make you an outlier. That proves that women can show up boldly, take up space and believe in themselves without apology. Let's normalise that.

However, if you do experience impostor syndrome, just know you are not alone, and strap in. The moment you decide to go for more — more impact, more visibility, more leadership — is often when the voice of self-doubt gets loud. Remember this isn't because you're underqualified, but because you're evolving.

Impostor syndrome in action

A year ago, I stood in front of a room full of brilliant women in the technology department at a global retail brand. These weren't juniors; they were leaders, architects, developers, women building platforms, managing systems, and shaping the future of the digital infrastructure.

As I opened the session and introduced the topic of impostor syndrome, the energy shifted, not because the concept was unfamiliar, but because it was intimately understood. I shared a story with these women that I now want to share with you, because it illustrates perfectly how impostor syndrome can show up.

Let's call the woman in the story Jen.

Jen is an experienced software developer, respected by her peers, known for her problem-solving skills and a go-to in her team. But when her company introduced a new technology stack, Jen's confidence began to wobble. Impostor syndrome showed up in the following ways:

- She started comparing herself to colleagues who seemed to adapt faster.

- She held back in meetings, convinced someone else could say what she was thinking better.

- She avoided most coding tasks, sticking with what felt familiar.

- She was still showing up ... but she was shrinking inside.

That's what impostor syndrome does. It whispers in your ear and gets in your head — and its favourite phrase is, 'You're not good enough'.

As I shared Jen's story, I could see the women in the room all relating. So, we got practical. We talked about what to do when self-doubt shows up, and I shared the three practical strategies I also want to share with you now — because once you learn to recognise impostor syndrome for what it is and understand how to deal with it, it loses its grip and no longer gets to run the show.

First, name it to tame it

I say this often: Once you're aware of something, you have the power to change it. Because you can't shift what you don't first acknowledge. If you're unaware of the self-doubt running in the background, you'll assume the thoughts running through your head are the truth. If you don't recognise impostor syndrome for what it is, you'll internalise it as fact. If you're unaware of your inner dialogue, you'll start believing every negative thought that enters your mind, and those unchecked beliefs will quietly shape your life and career.

Awareness gives you a choice. And choice gives you power.

Impostor syndrome thrives in secrecy. Psychologist Dr Valerie Young, a leading researcher on impostor syndrome, says that simply labelling the experience helps disrupt the pattern and reduce its emotional hold. The moment you name what's happening — simply saying to yourself, 'This is impostor syndrome' — you create distance between you and the thought. You can move from identifying with it ('I'm not good enough') to observing it ('Oh, that's my brain trying to protect me again').

One of my favourite examples of this came from Career Confidence podcast guest Cathryn Arnold, who talked with me about her experience as a chief technology officer. Her career journey was extraordinary, taking her from the call centre to leading the technology department for one of Australia's biggest companies, but it wasn't without impostor syndrome showing up along the way.

Every time Cathryn stepped up into a new role, she would begin to doubt her abilities. Instead of believing everything her inner critic told her, however, she decided to give her impostor voice a name: Kirsty. Whenever this voice of self-doubt crept in, telling her she wasn't ready, that she'd mess up, that she didn't belong, she'd respond with something like, 'Oh, Kirsty's back. She's trying to keep me small again. Thanks for your concern, but I've got this'.

It sounds playful, but it's powerful. Cathryn created space between her and the fear by naming her inner critic. This allowed her to respond with compassion and authority rather than letting that voice run wild in her head.

Ever since this conversation with Cathryn, I have used this hack in my own life. I call my own inner critic 'Sue', and when that voice pops up, I call it out: 'Ah, there's Sue again. I see you, but you're not in charge today'.

By doing this, I have begun to retrain my brain to recognise what's happening and choose a different response. And that's where confidence begins — not in eliminating the voice, but in refusing to obey it.

I now invite you to name your inner critic. Use this name to create distance between you and the limiting voice in your head. Take a moment to do that now.

Second, take action before you feel ready

Action is how you outgrow impostor syndrome — not by waiting for the doubt to disappear, but by going for your dreams and goals, and letting confidence catch up. This goes back to the myth I discuss in chapter 1 about waiting to feel confident before taking the next step. Remember — first, you must have the courage to act.

When I reflect on my life so far, I can honestly say that I have never felt ready. I didn't feel ready to move to Australia at 23, transition my career into recruitment, start my business, step on any stage, start a podcast, run events or even write this book.

Before every one of these bold moves, I was full of nerves, doubt and impostor syndrome — and, if I am honest, in the early days a lot of naivety! But I have learned most of my new skills from doing and taking action, not by waiting for permission or the perfect time. Have I made mistakes? Absolutely, enough to fill a book of their own. But I wouldn't change a single one. Every setback, every wrong turn, every uncomfortable lesson has shaped me into the woman I am today.

If I had listened to that inner critic or, as I now like to call her, 'Sue', I wouldn't be living the life I am now. I wouldn't be running my own business, speaking on stages or helping hundreds of people transform their careers.

When it comes to taking bold action, I have three simple questions I ask myself anytime I want to make an important decision in my life. These three questions are:

1. What is the best case?

2. What is the worst case?

3. What is the likely case?

So often, when we are contemplating bold decisions across any stage of life, we can jump to the worst-case scenario and quickly talk ourselves out of doing something that could help improve our lives. On the other hand, we can also exaggerate the good bits, setting big expectations of what we would like to achieve, only to realise that they may not, in fact, be achievable, leading to disappointment if things don't play out how we wanted them to.

Between these two extremes is the likely case — the 'meet-in-the-middle' position, the realisation that everything has pros and cons, good and bad, and that life is not a linear path; it comes full of highs and lows and everything in between.

To illustrate how this middle ground looks, let me share a personal story of starting my business, CH Solutions. I have never told this story before, so I hope it inspires you to take action and start before you feel ready.

My bold move from employee to business owner

My best friend, Pam, and I were in Bali. We had just spent six nights soaking up the vibes and were feeling relaxed as we sat in our villa on a warm evening, sipping a gin and tonic. Bliss!

We had worked together for the past few years at a recruitment agency and were both flying high in our careers. As we sat there, knowing that the holiday was coming to an end, we began to discuss work and realised neither of us was particularly excited to go back the following Monday.

The truth was we felt like we were cruising, that we had hit a glass ceiling, and weren't sure where the progression was. Pam had also expressed an interest in stepping up into a management role and had been met with a question that no woman should ever be asked: 'Was she planning

(continued)

on extending her family?' I remember her telling me this and almost choking on my gin and tonic!

Now on my second double gin (with Pam's pour, it was more like a triple), I said something that momentarily stunned both of us: 'Pam, why don't we start our own agency?'

She looked at me and said nothing. After a long pause, she said, 'Georgie, that's my dream'.

'Well, let's do it then', I responded.

Feeling excited, we began discussing the name, vision and mission of the company. We chatted all night and finally fell asleep, dreaming of all the possibilities.

The next morning, not feeling too fresh from the night before, we began packing up to leave. It was a busy morning, as it always is when you have a plane to catch, so we didn't have much time to discuss our business idea.

Once we got to the airport and grabbed a very strong coffee, we began to discuss the idea again. This time around, it was a very different conversation. Overthinking and catastrophising had well and truly begun. Pam's biggest concern was she had a very young daughter and, even though she had a very supportive husband, she was concerned about us not making enough money and what that might mean for her family.

For me, I was worried that I had just stretched myself to buy my first home, and had no savings left and a mortgage to pay. I was also earning great money after years of building my reputation and client base, so the idea of starting from zero made me nervous.

At this point, we were both full of doubt and our inner critic was running the show. Who were we to start a business?

Neither of us had studied business or finance before. We didn't have a fancy degree and hadn't gone to a prestigious school. We didn't have a clue about where to begin or how much it would cost to start, let alone run a business.

Without realising it, we were experiencing impostor syndrome and focusing on the worst-case scenario, rhyming off all the things that could go wrong — all the 'ifs, buts and maybes' our minds were creating for us.

Thankfully, my husband, Kyle, was sitting there listening to all this and said, 'Why don't you just register the business and take the first step? You don't need to start right away, but you can just register the name and start when you're ready'. He then went on to say he could build the website for us and help out where he could. (Side note: Kyle has always been my biggest supporter, and we all need our cheerleaders. He was one of them on that day and has continued to be ever since.)

By the time we landed back in Melbourne, we had a name for the business CH Solutions (based on the initials of mine and Pam's last names, Caldwell and Hubbard — not very creative, I know!) and had registered the business.

This is a key lesson in taking the first step before you feel ready. It doesn't matter how small the step is; what matters is that you take it. So next time you have an idea or an urge to try something new, do something in that moment and just begin.

Driving home from the airport, I felt the excitement kick in again. I had gone over all the worst-case scenarios and, to be completely honest, they really weren't that bad. Sure, them all actually happening would not be ideal, but I had the evidence from six years in recruitment that told me

(continued)

I could be successful. When it comes to the worst-case scenario, you are going to think it regardless. Speaking it or writing it out releases its power over you and helps you gain perspective. You may even realise, as I did that day, that the worst-case scenario really isn't the end of the world and you would get through it, no matter how uncomfortable it may feel in the moment. Remember the regrets of the dying I shared in chapter 1 and how, when you reach the end of your life, it likely won't be your missteps you dwell on, but the missed opportunities.

I then began thinking big. What was the best-case scenario?

I wrote down what the first three, six and 12 months could look like, including the big accounts I would break into and how successful we would be. Within 12 months, I would own the best and brightest agency in Melbourne, and have a team of top recruitment agents who all wanted to work for CH Solutions. I felt like a rock star!

However good this all sounded in theory, I knew that setting crazy high expectations, and then not being able to achieve them, would only lead to disappointment. This, in turn, would erode confidence and self-belief and lead to feeling like an impostor.

Having fallen into this trap too many times before, I sat down, grabbed my journal and asked myself to find the middle ground. What was the likely case?

The likely case was that we would have a very strict 'non-compete clause', meaning I would not be able to work with any of my current clients for at least six months, and neither would Pam. So we would have to work incredibly hard to build a new client base.

For the first three months, we would likely do one or two placements, meaning we would take a very small salary, if any, because we would have to reinvest in the business for marketing and branding. To help pay the mortgage, Kyle and I would need to rent out the spare room in our home to ease the financial pressure.

At the six-month mark, we would be making more traction and be able to pay ourselves a bit more to cover our day-to-day expenses, but wouldn't be able to afford luxuries such as breakfast and dinners out or holidays.

At 12 months, we would have begun to establish ourselves in the Melbourne market, have a handful of clients we were working with, and could begin paying ourselves enough to have a few extra luxuries back in life and potentially be looking to make our first hire.

To be honest, this 'likely case' is pretty much exactly what the first 12 months of our business looked like. I have never worked so hard in my entire life, but looking back, I would not change a thing.

As I reflect on starting CH Solutions and the journey Pam and I went through together, I feel incredibly proud of what we achieved. It was not easy, but it was worth it. As I sit here now, writing this book, I am so grateful for younger Georgie, the risk she took to start, and the amount of work she put in. Had she listened to the inner critic or focused on the worst-case scenario, she never would have taken the action and taken the first step. Alternatively, if she had focused on the best-case scenario, she could have lost motivation when her expectations weren't met.

I am approaching eight years in business, and it has not been an easy ride, but I know one thing is for sure. I would have regretted the decision not to act and, as I've mentioned, that is my biggest fear.

I hope my story drives home the message that you will never feel ready. By using these three questions to uncover the best case, worst case and likely case, you will begin to feel more confident in making bold moves that could profoundly impact your life and career.

So, if you have a dream or a goal you want to achieve, have the courage to act before you feel ready — your future self will thank you for it.

'But Georgie', I hear you ask, 'what if I fail?' To that, I respond simply by stating, I do not believe in failure — only failure to learn and grow. I have 'failed' at many things, but without this failure, I would not have learned the incredibly valuable lessons that have helped me reach my next level of success.

Third, invest in your growth

Confidence isn't about knowing everything; it's about trusting your ability to learn and figure things out as you go. When it comes to overcoming self-doubt and building confidence, I believe it is absolutely critical to continue expanding your knowledge.

When you continue to upskill, take a course, read, ask questions or seek mentorship, you're helping to shut down self-doubt. You're telling your brain, 'I might not know this yet, but I'm capable of figuring it out'.

On my Career Confidence podcast, I spoke with Sheena Peeters, a leader in the tech space, who shared something that's stayed with me ever since. She told me she was 'never done learning'.

Sheena has built an incredible career across multiple sectors, including tech, criminal law and strategy, and her secret to success has been constant upskilling. And she hasn't continued to upskill because she was behind, but because she was curious, and because she wanted to lead with insight, not just instinct.

She told me that staying open to new knowledge — whether it's AI, cloud computing or complex legal frameworks — has helped her stay confident and credible in rooms full of experts.

'You don't have to know everything', she said, 'but you have to know enough to ask the right questions, and then be willing to learn the answers'.

Sheena's story reminds us that confidence isn't about knowing it all; it's about backing ourselves and believing we are capable of learning what we need to know — and that mindset is available to all of us. Impostor syndrome often tells us, 'You don't belong here', or 'You're not as capable as everyone else'. One of the most powerful ways to quiet that voice is to work on yourself, not because you're not good enough, but because you're committed to your growth. Trust me when I say that every time you choose to learn, you're reminding yourself that you're not stuck, you're in motion.

Here's what I want you to remember as we reach the end of this chapter. Feeling like an impostor doesn't mean you are one or that you don't belong; it means you're in the unknown. This space is often where growth happens. You don't outgrow impostor syndrome by achieving more; you learn to move with it. Call it out and give your inner critic a name to create space between you and the voice inside your head. When doubt shows up, ask yourself: what's the best, worst and most likely scenario? These questions alone can unlock action, and stop you from talking yourself out of a bold move. Finally, keep learning, because confidence grows when you stay curious and back yourself, even when you don't feel ready.

Rewrite your inner narrative to prepare for your next bold move

Before we move on to the next chapter, it's time to rewrite your story and change your internal dialogue. Take the first step in overcoming impostor syndrome so you can prepare to make your bold move without the inner critic running the show.

Grab your journal, device or notepad and complete the following:

1. Give your inner critic a name, so it loses power over you.

2. Identify one bold move you want to take but haven't because of fear.

3. Call out the fear and ask yourself what the worst-case scenario is of going for this bold move.

4. What is the best-case scenario for pursuing this bold move?

5. What is the likely case scenario for this bold move?

6. Take immediate action, however small, and get in motion.

Chapter 3

Building career resilience and adaptability

In this chapter, I explore two skills that will shape how you show up in the future of work: resilience and adaptability. These aren't 'nice-to-haves'. They're crucial skills for navigating change, handling pressure and making decisions when things feel uncertain.

Resilience is about getting back up when things don't go to plan. Adaptability is about staying open, learning quickly and adjusting without losing your direction. You don't need to master either of these skills overnight, but you do need to begin building them now.

So in the following sections, I walk you through a simple, practical way to break habits that no longer serve you and replace them with ones that do. I also provide tools to move through change and uncertainty with more clarity and control.

The world of work is changing *fast*

The world of work is more volatile than ever. Restructuring, AI disruption, and a complete shift in how and where we work are all happening at lightning speed.

When I reflect on the last decade of my recruitment career, everything has changed. I used to commute to the office five days a week. Now, I can work from anywhere thanks to advances in technology, email on my phone, faster internet, and Zoom or Microsoft Teams for online meetings. Posting job ads used to be the norm, but now LinkedIn gives me real-time data on who's open to work, so I don't have to wait around for applications to come in. Applicant tracking systems (ATSs) then make it easier to manage roles and track where every candidate is in the process. I can even use AI to write job descriptions, record meetings, reach out to potential talent, and create marketing copy and reports. Many of these tools only emerged recently, and they've had a profound impact on how I work.

How much change have you seen in your career over the past decade? Chances are the way you approach work looks completely different.

According to the World Economic Forum, by 2030, the average person's daily life will be unrecognisable compared to 2020. I'm not saying that to scare you, I'm saying it to prepare you.

The future of work is also going to look wildly different, and it's coming faster than most of us would like. According to 2023 research by McKinsey (published in their report 'Generative AI and the future of work in America'), up to 30 per cent of the tasks we do today could be automated by 2030. That's not some futuristic, sci-fi prediction; it's the world we're stepping into, and it's happening fast. A 2024 study by McKinsey focusing on AI and the future of work in Australia stated that 1.3 million Australian workers may need to shift into new roles over the next five years.

However, before you spiral, let's look at the full picture. According to a 2020 report by the Australian Computer Society (ACS), up to 5.6 million new jobs could be created by 2035, with 25 per cent of these new jobs in technology related roles. This highlights the potential for significant employment growth if Australia invests in re-skilling and workforce transformation.

So, yes, the world of work is changing fast, but it's not all doom and gloom. This is your opportunity to pivot, re-skill and carve out a career that's secure, energising and future-ready. The most important thing to remember is that the people who will thrive won't be the ones with the most experience. They'll be the ones who are the most resilient and adaptable.

These two skills are becoming essential in this new world of work, so let's break them down.

Resilience in a world of change

According to Oxford Languages, resilience is defined as, 'The capacity to withstand or to recover quickly from difficulties; toughness'. That's how the dictionary defines it. But how does it look in our day-to-day lives?

Resilience is:

- choosing to get out of bed in the mornings and work on your future when it would be easier to sleep in

- hitting 'send' on the job application even after three rejections

- walking into a room where you feel like an impostor, holding your head high and backing yourself anyway

- hearing no and choosing to go again

- having the quiet courage to stay committed when no-one's watching or cheering you on

- saying, 'Today was rough', and still going again tomorrow

- being kind to yourself in the chaos, and still doing the thing

- trusting that, even when it's hard, you're not going to let this be the end of your story.

Resilience doesn't look like perfection. It looks like grit, grace and getting back up, again and again. The best part is it's not something you either have or you don't. It's something you build, choice by choice, day by day.

Adapting quickly

Now let's look at the definition for adaptability. Again according to Oxford Languages, adaptability is defined as, 'The quality of being able to adjust to new conditions'. Nice, simple definition. But how does this play out in our lives?

Adaptability in real life isn't about being perfect; it's about being flexible. It's what kicks in when your role suddenly changes, your strategy falls short, or that 'five-year plan' you were so sure of no longer fits.

Adaptability looks like:

- being open to learning a new system at work without complaining, and trying out a different way of working when the old one stops delivering

- staying calm when the unexpected lands in your lap

- shifting gears instead of shutting down, even if it means starting again or letting go of control

- staying curious, staying open and being able to lean into discomfort instead of retreating from it.

Adaptability is less about having all the answers and more about being willing to evolve, experiment and move forward, even when the path looks different from what you imagined.

Both adaptability and resilience will matter more than ever over the next decade of work. These skills will carry you through. When priorities shift, plans change and things get hard, these qualities will help you stay steady and keep moving forward. You don't need to have all the answers to stand out, but you will need to navigate change, stay open, and keep showing up anyway.

Mone's bold career pivot: From nursing to cybersecurity

One of the standout conversations from my Career Confidence podcast that showcases adaptability and resilience in action was one I had with Mone, who made the bold leap from nursing into cybersecurity, a booming field with tremendous growth potential.

Mone didn't just 'fall into' cybersecurity; she earned her place through sheer determination, grit and resilience. After more than a decade in nursing, including in trauma care, emergency services and the military, she began noticing how much tech surrounded her—including pacemakers, insulin pumps and ventilators. She had no idea how these life-saving tools were protected from cyber threats, and that lack of understanding unsettled her. She felt compelled to do something about it.

So she started where many people stop: Google. She immersed herself in research, studying cybersecurity basics, certifications and LinkedIn forums. She reached out to people in the industry and asked if she could chat with them about what they did. She also enrolled in eLearning through CompTIA to gain IT certifications.

With three kids and working fulltime, her time was limited. Mone got up before 5 am every day to study before the household woke up. She poured hours into learning and preparing for the CompTIA exams. Despite her hard work, she failed one. But instead of quitting, she reframed it.

'It just meant I needed to study a little harder', she said. 'I didn't see it as a failure, I saw it as feedback.'

Eventually, a CEO she'd messaged on LinkedIn reached out. He'd followed her journey, saw her passion and transferable skills, and offered her a role in his cybersecurity company.

At first, she hesitated. The impostor syndrome crept in. Was she really ready? Eventually, she said yes and entered a whole new world. She was a beginner again, surrounded by unfamiliar jargon. But, rather than become overwhelmed, she relied on the same habits that got her there: curiosity, adaptability, resilience and consistency. Every day, she wrote down what she didn't understand and every night she researched until it clicked.

Today, Mone is thriving, not just because she made a bold leap but also because she never stopped learning.

It's a real-life example showcasing that resilience isn't about having all the answers. It's about having the courage to start anyway.

Building career grit

If you plan to stay in the workforce for the next 10 to 30 years, here's the reality: you will likely face rejection, redundancy or failure at some point. It's almost unavoidable unless you move off-grid to tend a veggie patch fulltime.

Throughout my own career, I've gotten very used to hearing the word 'no':

- No, Georgie, we're not hiring.

- No, Georgie, we don't use agencies.

- No, Georgie, we're not looking for more candidates.

- No, Georgie, we can't work with you; we've got a preferred supplier list.

The list goes on. I've been ghosted, hung up on and even bluntly told to F off. Yep, the life of a recruiter.

In the early days, this rejection really shook me. I'd go home questioning if I was good enough. I had high levels of anxiety, because I was always piling on the pressure and listening to that inner critic. Back then, I didn't have a name for her (like I do now — refer to the previous chapter), so she often ruled the roost.

What kept me going even when I felt like giving up (which was multiple times a week) was the vision I had for my career. I could see a future in recruitment. I loved helping people get work and hearing how the new employee was bringing huge value to a small business or a big project.

I remember the moment things shifted. It had been one of those days when everything felt like it was falling apart. Two candidates turned down offers, one didn't show up to their interview and, to top it off, a client I'd spent days sourcing talent for decided to pull the role altogether. A tough day in recruitment! I walked home to my apartment in Melbourne's CBD and, instead of turning on some mind-numbing TV or opening a bottle of wine to ease my frustration, I sat down and took a deep breath. Intuitively, I knew something had to change internally before anything was going to change externally. I needed clarity and to reconnect with why I was in this new career. I grabbed my journal and started asking myself some better questions:

- What does success look like for me — not just on paper, but in my day to day?

- What am I willing to do differently from this point forward?

- What part of the job do I want to master — sourcing, client strategy, negotiation?

- Where am I playing small?

A pattern I have recognised in my life is that whenever I feel stuck, it's not because I haven't been capable, it's because I am focusing on the wrong things and asking the wrong questions. Better questions lead to better answers, which have shifted my perspective, sparked new ideas and moved me forward.

Once I had sat with these questions and taken some time to let the answers sink in, I asked myself the most important question of all: *Who do I need to become in order to make my career goals a reality?*

That one question changed everything, because answering it revealed not just what I was doing wrong, but also what I was focusing on — the story I was telling myself and how I was showing up.

If I wanted different results, I knew I couldn't keep operating with the same habits that had gotten me stuck in the first place. I had to be honest and understand what would help me move forward, and what was quietly holding me back.

Welcome to the bold gap

At this moment in my career, I was right in the thick of what I now call the 'bold gap'. This was the uncomfortable space between who I was and who I wanted to be — and it was also where I needed to be the most resilient and adaptable.

When I found myself stuck in this gap, I asked myself two questions:

1. What do I need to *stop* doing?

2. What do I need to *start* doing?

I know this sounds so simple, but answering these two basic questions enabled one of the most significant shifts. The lists I created in response made me instantly aware of all the habits that were not serving me, and all the new habits I needed to adopt to make a difference. Awareness without action won't move the needle, and that's why this exercise is so powerful.

On my 'stop doing' list, I wrote:

- Stop complaining to my colleagues about how tough this job is.

- Stop comparing myself to co-workers.

- Stop staying up late watching rubbish TV.

- Stop focusing on things outside of my control.

- Stop picking up non-work calls and texts during the day.

- Stop drinking energy drinks.

- Stop skipping lunch breaks.

- Stop saying yes to everyone in the office.

- Stop holding back ideas in meetings.

- Stop speaking to every candidate who isn't right for the role.

- Stop aimlessly scrolling Facebook during work hours.

The list made one thing clear: my daily habits were leaking energy, focus and potential. These weren't just small distractions; they were the invisible barriers between me and the outcomes I wanted.

Then came the 'start doing' list, a blueprint for who I needed to become:

- Start going to bed before 10 pm and aim for eight hours sleep.

- Start waking up at 6 am to get to the gym.

- Start writing a list of daily priorities the night before.

- Start drinking more water.

- Start reading personal development books.

- Start shadowing a senior consultant in the office.

- Start taking real lunch breaks to reset.

- Start limiting distractions and closing extra tabs.

- Start reaching out to ten companies a week.

- Start connecting with 100 IT professionals on LinkedIn weekly.

- Start dressing like the professional I wanted to be.

This was the beginning of a new chapter.

Now, there is no denying it was a big shift, and I had no idea at that time just how hard it would be to transform from who I was in that moment into who I wanted to become, but I knew I had to try. If I didn't, the career I wanted to master would never become a reality. I took radical responsibility and slowly but surely began to move away from the bad habits and instead stack the new ones.

The results spoke for themselves. In under three years, I went from struggling and underperforming to a top-performing recruitment consultant. Sure, it took time and, no, it wasn't easy. I had days when the self-doubt crept back in, when I slipped into old habits or felt like I wasn't getting anywhere. But I noticed it and didn't spiral, gave myself grace, and kept going.

This is where adaptability and resilience come in. They give you the ability to shift gears when things don't go to plan, to stay open, adjust and keep moving forward, even when things get hard. You can notice the wobble without falling apart. And you can feel the fear, the frustration and the failure, and still show up again and again.

The best part is that, like confidence, adaptability and resilience can be built. They're not something you have or don't have. The amount of resilience I now have has come through tough times, when I have had to continue to show up for myself, even though things felt impossible. On those days when lying in bed all day would have been the easy and comfortable option but, instead, I've chosen to get up, get dressed and face the day — those are times I've built resilience.

Because these skills aren't built during the wins. They're built during the in-between, in the gap — in the early mornings, the awkward conversations and the quiet moments when no-one's watching. They're built during the times you choose to try again.

When you find yourself in a season of change or facing a challenge or uncertain of your next bold move, see it as a sign that you are growing. Know that you are in the bold gap. In this space, you are going to come up against yourself, and you are going to have to dig deep and tool up. This in-between space — the stretch between who you were and who you're becoming — is unfamiliar territory. And it's perhaps the toughest ground you'll ever walk on.

Being in the bold gap is like standing on a rope bridge between two cliffs. On one side is the comfort of who you used to be — including your old habits, identity and safety net. On the other side is your future self — stronger, more aligned, but not fully in reach yet. The bridge is wobbly and exposed, and can sometimes feel like it's not even going to get you to where you want to go. The following figure highlights all the emotions that can emerge — and that need to be navigated — when you find yourself in the bold gap.

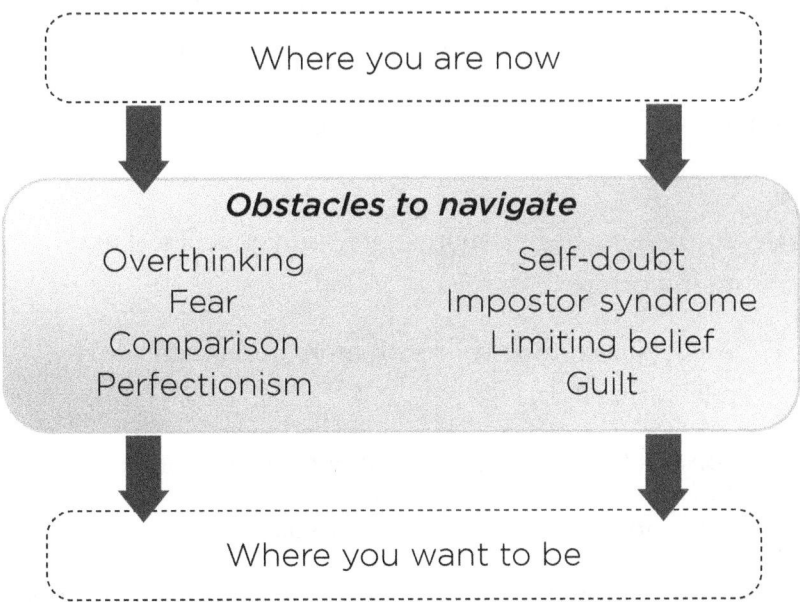

The bold gap between where you are and where you want to be

Despite these obstacles, that space of the bold gap — that uncertain, shaky, messy middle — is where adaptability comes in and resilience is built. It's also where 90 per cent of people give up, think this is too hard, and return to who they used to be. This is the easy option for sure, but in this world of change, it can't be your thought process.

Navigating the bold gap

After experiencing the bold gap early in my recruitment career, I've since found myself in this uncertain space more times than I can count. If you're striving for more in your career, chances are you will find yourself there too. It's that place between who you used to be in your professional life and who you're working hard to become. You've left behind the old roles, old habits or outdated goals, but you haven't yet arrived at your next level.

If you're wondering if you're at this stage, ask yourself if you can relate to any of the following:

- You're not a beginner anymore, but you still feel like an impostor.

- You're questioning your path more often than you're celebrating it.

- You feel like you're doing a lot but not getting 'there'.

- Your motivation fluctuates day to day.

- You're tempted to go back to what was easy, comfortable or familiar.

- You're constantly comparing yourself to people further ahead.

- You find yourself stuck in 'waiting mode' — waiting for clarity, confidence or permission.

I can relate to everything on the list, and maybe you can too. The good thing is, now you are aware of the bold gap, you have the power to change it.

Ultimately, you will find yourself in the bold gap when you move past your comfort zone or are in a season of change. Trying something new is always going to feel uncomfortable. This is where resilience and adaptability are needed more than ever. To thrive in the future of work, you need to be able to lean into this discomfort and navigate the in-between, moving yourself from where you are to where you want to be. Change doesn't happen overnight. It takes time and patience, and consistently showing up and doing the work.

Navigating the bold gap to launch my first event

I found myself back in the bold gap when I decided to launch my first-ever event — a women in tech initiative I planned to call 'Sisterhood Socials'. I had a strong 'why' for creating this event — I was fed up with going to technology networking events and being one of the only women in the room. I wanted to create a safe space where women could come together with their male allies, meet like-minded career professionals and learn something new.

I had never run an event before, but having been to a tonne of networking events and conferences over the years, I thought, *I'm going to give this a go*. I sat down and got clear on how I wanted the event to look. As well as

(continued)

creating a safe and welcoming environment, I also wanted the event to be inspiring and educational. I decided I would run a three-person panel to get a broad range of thoughts and opinions on topics I knew women especially would be interested in. I didn't want it to be a basic meet-up with beer and pizza, so I knew it would have to be in a space with a nice bar, catering for canapés, and big enough to network and then seat up to 60 people.

Once I had my list, I felt a sense of excitement. I started focusing on the best-case scenario: a room packed with like-minded career professionals, an amazing panel of female leaders, and a beautiful event space with delicious food and wine being served. I thought, *This is going to be fantastic.*

Unfortunately, that moment was fleeting. A few minutes later, the self-doubt began to kick in as my mind went straight to the worst-case scenario.

The thoughts went like this:

- *Who am I to run an event? I've never run an event before.*

- *Who would even speak at the event?*

- *Where would I host it? I don't know any event spaces.*

- *This is too much work, and I am busy enough.*

The list went on. But my biggest fear was this: *What if no-one turns up?* I had this image of an empty room with just me standing there. Talk about a disempowering thought!

In the previous chapter, I discussed identifying the best, worst and likely scenarios in any bold move. As you can see, you're likely going to do this regardless, which is why I got my notepad out and wrote it all down.

Once I got all the doomsday scenarios out of my head, and all of the incredibly exciting but slightly exaggerated ones, I moved on to the likely case.

Since this was the first time I had ever run an event, I wanted to enjoy the experience and not have my usual crazy expectations. I realised the likely case was that it would take a while to find the right space, book the speakers and organise all the promotions for it. I could utilise my network, reach out to those who run events and learn from them. For the first event, it would be great if 50 people attended. With my LinkedIn network and recruitment partners, this felt really achievable. I was also not looking to make any money from the event, so I thought I'd keep this really affordable and charge $20 a ticket. The more I wrote it out, the calmer and clearer I felt.

I began by ringing around event spaces, gathering prices and availability. Once I had a shortlist, I booked a time to see the venues as soon as possible.

I then reached out to a number of C-suite women in my network who were working in the technology space, asking if they would be interested in being on the panel. A big part of my motivation for running these events was to encourage more women to consider careers in tech, while also inspiring those already in the industry to keep upskilling and step confidently into senior positions and leadership roles. I'm a big believer that we can't be what we can't see, and I knew just how much representation mattered. When women see others who look like them succeeding, it doesn't just plant a seed; it gives them permission to believe it's possible for them too.

(continued)

To my delight, the women I reached out to said yes. Once I had spoken to them all and heard their enthusiasm, I remember thinking, *Wow. Now I have to do this.*

It all seemed to be going well, but I was about to enter the messy and uncertain bold gap!

The following week, I jumped on the train with Pam into Melbourne CBD to view some venues. I had a vision in my mind for how I wanted it all to look and feel. All the venues had looked great on paper, so I thought this was going to be easy.

When we entered the first event space, my heart sank. It was dark and dingy, with no natural light. There was no space for the panel or the 50 chairs we'd need. Oh dear. Maybe this would be harder than I thought.

The next space was beautiful. I knew it could be outside of our budget, but I thought it was good to feel inspired and have something to aim for. The space could host up to 250 people, it felt big and would be a stretch for our first event. Boldly, I asked if the price was negotiable (if you don't ask, you don't get) but, unfortunately, it wasn't due to the high demand. I decided, budget aside, it was just a bit too big for our first one, and I didn't want to stress myself out trying to sell hundreds of tickets. (I would later discover this was the right choice.)

We had one more venue to view before lunch. Again, there was no natural light, and it felt more like a club than a professional networking space.

Pam and I began to panic. Could we do this? Could we afford a venue that matched our vision? Could we get over 100 people to come to our first event? I really didn't want to end the day without having found our space.

At 3 pm, we were ready to meet another venue manager. I crossed my fingers and jumped in the lift. When the doors opened, I saw the perfect space. I started to feel excited again. There was a nice bar area as you walked in, enough space to network, and enough room for 50 chairs in front of the panel. They even arranged all the catering. We booked the space immediately and celebrated with a glass of bubbles before heading home.

Little did I know the gap was about to get wider!

With the speakers and venue all sorted, we began to design the marketing material and got the tickets ready to sell via Humanitix. We were pumped. The event was four weeks away, so we decided to promote it early to ensure we had enough time to sell all the tickets.

The next morning, we announced the event on LinkedIn. Pam and I had a busy day of meetings ahead, so I posted a link to the event page and got on with the day. On the drive home after a long day of one-on-ones with clients, I decided to call my husband, Kyle, to see how many tickets we had sold.

I said to Pam, 'I reckon we've sold at least 20 by now'.

Kyle picked up and, after a quick debrief of the day, I asked, 'So, how many have we sold then?'

He paused, and then said a sentence I'll never forget: 'We've sold three'.

Well, within seconds, I went from 'oh dear' to absolute fits of hysterics. Pam was driving and was laughing so hard that she had mascara running down her face. Luckily, a service station was in sight, so we pulled in and belly laughed for a good few minutes.

(continued)

Poor Kyle had no idea what was happening, but he's used to my and Pam's outbursts.

What I hadn't accounted for was that we were coming out of a period of extended lockdowns, and many people were still out of practice or even a little anxious about attending in-person events and social gatherings.

Suddenly, the giggles disappeared, and I was left feeling a little concerned, to say the least. Then the spiral began — and that image of me standing in an empty room reappeared in my mind.

At this stage, it would have been easy to turn back. We hadn't paid for anything yet, and I knew the speakers would understand. For a moment, I seriously considered it.

But then I remembered why this was important to me. I also remembered that this was all new, and so also where all the growth was.

The next morning, resilience kicked in and I sprang into action. I wrote an email to our recruitment database, inviting them to the event. Then I picked up the phone and started calling our clients, encouraging them to bring their teams along. Everyone seemed keen and asked for the invite to circulate internally.

I posted again on LinkedIn and messaged people in my network who I thought would be interested. By the end of the week, we'd sold 30 tickets, a much stronger start. Over the following weeks, I kept up the momentum, promoting the event across social media and reaching out personally to my network.

All of this was happening alongside my regular role at CH Solutions and the everyday demands of recruitment. It was exhausting at times and took up a lot of my headspace. But I was determined. I wanted the event to be a success, and I knew there was no easy button. I also knew that success wasn't going to come from posting once and waiting. It was going to come from showing up, following through and doing the unglamorous work behind the scenes.

From all the constant promotions and outreach, three days before the event, we'd ended up selling 60 tickets! I was delighted.

The day of the event, I woke up at 5 am full of excitement. It had been a big and full four weeks, so I wanted to enjoy the day and the experience of running my first event. I had to be up and out of the house early, because I had a couple of meetings in the city.

On the commute in at 8 am, my phone pinged with a message from one of the panellists. She wasn't feeling great and wasn't sure if she could make it. My stomach tightened and my body felt tense. This threw out the whole panel. I had already written all the questions and sent them through to the speakers, and everything flowed so well.

I caught myself beginning to spiral, but instead of getting stuck in the worst-case scenario, I jumped into problem-solving mode. I called the panellist and said I hoped she felt better, and requested that she please confirm by midday if she wasn't able to make it, so I could try to arrange a new speaker to take her place.

Instead of being frustrated about the situation, I needed to be adaptable.

I went to the list of people who were attending that night and saw some talented and senior career professionals

(continued)

would be in the crowd. I thought, *Okay, maybe I could see if one of these women would step in.* I put their names and numbers into my phone.

I decided to give the panellist a few hours, because I could tell she really wanted to be there. If she truly wasn't well enough, my options would be to either get someone to fill her spot or run with two panellists. I was calling and texting like a madwoman to ensure the rest of the panel was good and, gratefully, they were.

I suddenly felt calm. I took a deep breath and thought, *Everything is going to be okay.*

Ten am rolled around and, as I walked out of my first meeting, I checked my phone. I had a lot of text messages. Eight people had texted to say they couldn't make it. Cue the vision of me and two panellists on stage, with an audience of five people and rows of empty chairs. My stomach tightened again, and the panic set in.

I still hadn't heard back from the speaker either. At this point, I was well and truly in the gap, but turning back wasn't an option. I had to accept what will be, will be, and remind myself that this was all a big learning curve. I remember saying to myself, 'Georgie, you can't control what happens next, but you can control how you respond'.

I took a deep breath and called the team. I asked them to send out an email to our newsletter list and reopen the ticket booking page. Then, I jumped back on LinkedIn and posted an update, letting people know a few spots had opened up due to last-minute cancellations, and they'd be available for a limited time.

I turned my phone on 'Do Not Disturb' and stepped into my next meeting. I came out and checked my phone afterwards and saw I had a missed call from the speaker. She'd left a voicemail saying she was feeling much better, and was going to make it!

I literally jumped up and down with sheer relief and joy.

Then I saw we'd sold five more tickets. I began to feel a huge weight lift off my shoulders and the excitement came back. What a roller-coaster.

Later that day, Pam, Kyle, the CH Solutions team and I made our way to the venue to get set up for the evening ahead. I went straight for the bar and ordered myself a glass of bubbles. I looked at Pam and said, 'No matter what happens from here, I'm going to lean in and enjoy this evening'.

And that's exactly what I did.

The whole night was so enjoyable from start to finish. Everyone who came brought amazing energy, and the room was electric. I remember being nervous before the panel started, but all the Toastmasters sessions paid off again, and the speakers made my job easy. Their answers to my questions were full of value, honesty and lots of humour. Lots of laughter, nods and smiles came from the audience, and I could tell everyone was enjoying themselves.

As the night came to a close, countless people came up to me to tell me it was a great event and ask when the next one would be, which elevated my excitement.

I looked around and saw people swapping numbers, connecting on LinkedIn, and organising coffee catch-ups. It honestly felt incredible. I knew this was the start of something important.

Reflecting now on the bold gap I found myself in before running my first event, here is what I know for sure:

- If I hadn't taken that very first step despite the doubt creeping in …

- If I'd turned back when the perfect venue didn't show up …

- If I'd pulled the pin after selling just three tickets …

- If I'd cancelled the whole thing on the day when it felt like everything was falling apart …

I would have missed out on what was waiting at the finish line. In that moment, standing there, looking around the room, I felt it: a deep, grounded sense of joy and pride. Nothing worth building comes easily, but if you start with the vision and the end in mind, it's always, always worth it.

Since that first event, the CH Solutions team and I have hosted eight more. The women who attend have gone on to secure new jobs, earn promotions, gain mentors and build meaningful friendships. I had no idea when I started just how much impact the Sisterhood Socials would have, but watching them grow and evolve has brought me immense joy.

And remember that big, luxurious event space I mentioned, the one that fits over 250 people? That's where we host the events now. In fact, they've built so much momentum that we've gained sponsorship from some of Australia's top companies who want to support the movement.

Imagine if I had given up — if I'd told myself it was too hard, or focused on the worst-case scenario. It's fair to say none of this would have happened.

We often only see the tip of the iceberg when it comes to someone arriving at their destination. We see the polished event, the job promotion or the big moment of success. But what we often don't see is the messy middle — the gap, the uncertainty, the setbacks and the days when it all feels too hard. That part usually doesn't make it to the highlight reel, but trust me that it is where the real growth happens.

And the truth is the bold gap isn't something you can avoid. It's part of the journey if you're chasing anything that really matters to you. Whether you're working towards a career goal, getting healthier, a new idea or a different version of yourself, it will come with its challenges.

But by continuing to show up despite the doubts and despite the detours, the momentum starts to build. You begin to build self-trust, which is a huge part of building self-belief and confidence. You begin to stack the evidence that you can do hard things — that you can back yourself and can overcome challenges.

Remember — resilience isn't built when everything is going well. And adaptability doesn't grow when you're comfortable. Both are built in the gap and the in-between moments when things feel shaky, but you choose to keep going anyway.

So if you're in the bold gap right now, keep this thought with you: you're not broken, you're becoming. This is the part of the journey that shapes you. Take what you've learned in this chapter and turn it into action. Use the following exercise to craft your stop/start list, trust yourself and start where you are. Because the version of you you're becoming is going to thank you for starting.

Work through your bold gap

If I hope you take one thing from this chapter, it's this: resilience and adaptability aren't qualities reserved for a select few. They're not things you're born with or things you magically 'unlock' when life is smooth sailing. They're *skills* — skills that are built through repetition, reflection and showing up even when it's hard.

To navigate your own bold gap, you can start small. Start where you are. Start messy if you have to. But just start. And the best way to start is with a stop/start list.

Grab your journal, device or notepad and create two columns — one titled 'Stop doing' and the other 'Start doing'.

To help you complete the 'Stop doing' column, ask yourself:

- What habits are draining my energy or focus?

- Where am I playing small, avoiding action or making excuses?

- What's distracting me from the career (and life) I actually want?

Be honest in your responses. No-one else is reading this. Call yourself out. This is your chance to see where your time, energy and mindset are going and what's no longer serving you.

To complete the 'Start doing' column, ask yourself:

- What actions would bring me closer to the career and life I want?

- What mindset shifts or habits would help me build more resilience and adaptability?

- What am I not doing yet, but deep down know I should be?

In your responses for this column, think progress, not perfection. You're not trying to flip your whole life overnight; you're choosing one or two things to start doing differently this week.

The following table outlines how to organise your stop/start list, and includes some examples of what each column might include.

Example stop/start list

Stop doing	Start doing
• Saying yes to things that don't align with my goals • Checking social media ten times a day • Comparing myself to co-workers • Talking myself out of trying something new	• Waking up 30 minutes earlier to plan my day and get movement in • Connecting with ten new people each week who I admire • Learning a new skill for ten minutes a day • Saying yes to things that scare (and excite) me

Chapter 4

Moving from overwhelmed to intentional

I n this chapter, I help you get intentional about one of your most valuable career tools: time. If you want to future-proof your career, the reality is you'll need to invest in learning, build new skills and stay open to evolving with the world of work. That takes focus, not just effort.

This might be one of the most confronting — but also one of the most empowering — chapters, because in the following sections I ask you to look at where your time really goes, what's helping you move forward and what might be holding you back.

It's time to step off the hamster wheel. Stop working more hours or making big sacrifices, and start using your time with more clarity and purpose. This is about getting smarter with your energy, not busier with your schedule. It's about breaking out of the 'busy trap' and carving a path that actually leads somewhere important, not somewhere urgent.

The busy trap

I've noticed a pattern in how people answer a question I ask daily: 'How are you?' Whether it's clients, candidates, friends or even a stranger at the dog park, the reply is almost always the same: 'Busy'. As a recruiter speaking with hundreds of professionals each week, I hear it constantly. It's automatic, and I used to be exactly the same.

Someone would ask, 'Hey, Georgie, how's things?'

And I'd smile, 'Oh, you know — just so busy lately!'

If a client called and asked how I was doing, I'd respond without thinking, 'Busy!'

Being busy became my brand and my default answer. I told myself it meant I was important, and made me look like I was in demand and doing well. But the truth was that business wasn't booming, and neither was my energy.

Despite the full calendar and constant activity, I was depleted. My days were packed, yet I was going to bed wondering what I had actually achieved. I was stuck in a cycle of reactive work, checking emails the moment they pinged, racing from task to task, saying yes to everything, and never pausing for breath. I felt like I was sprinting on a treadmill and had forgotten how to slow it down.

This wasn't just unproductive, it was unsustainable. I was anxious, overstimulated, and operating on caffeine, adrenaline and autopilot. I told myself I was 'just in a busy season and this is what starting a business looked like', but, in truth, 'busyness' had become a lifestyle.

Let me paint the picture in a little more detail. Back in the early days of CH Solutions, my mornings started before my feet even hit the floor: alarm, email, stress, scrolling and socials. Then the gym, the second coffee, a packed train ride filled with inbox refreshing, and a full day of candidate calls, meetings and screen time. No breaks, just more coffee, more emails and more noise. Evenings were no better, as I ate dinner with one eye on my inbox, my laptop open and my brain still in work mode. I'd have reality TV playing in the background, and still be refreshing my email.

Busy? Absolutely. Productive? Not really.

One Friday afternoon, I was sitting in my home office and reflecting on the week. I felt like it had been another busy week, but as I sat there looking at the jobs I had on my desk, I realised I had no interviews booked in for the following week, and I hadn't sent that many new candidates to my clients that week either. When you're in recruitment, CVs sent, interviews booked, new jobs to work and client meetings are all key metrics to measure, because these tasks are what lead to success. I started to ask myself, 'What did I actually accomplish this week?'

I realised I hadn't completed enough of the right activities to move my business forward. Sure, I'd made a lot of calls, answered emails and completed admin tasks, but I hadn't accomplished enough of the important activities I knew would get the results I wanted. That's when it hit me:

I wasn't working on the things that mattered most. I was stuck in the busy trap. At that moment, I knew something had to change. I needed to get intentional about what was important to me and come back to why I had started the business in the first place.

Dr Marny's bold realisation: When busy becomes a barrier

Realising I was stuck in the busy trap isn't unique to me, of course. On my Career Confidence podcast, I recently chatted with psychologist Dr Marny Lishman. She described spending years in a state of constant doing, equating a full calendar with progress and 'busy' with value.

She saw this in many of her patients too. So many professionals would arrive in her clinic completely exhausted and either on the verge of burnout or fully burned out. She began recognising a pattern she herself had fallen into.

'If my week wasn't packed, it felt like I wasn't doing enough', she told me.

But, despite all the doing, she'd reach Friday and ask, 'What did I actually achieve?' That question soon changed everything. Dr Marny started tracking her energy, not just her hours, and learned to protect space, not just fill it. She made peace with doing less, and started doing what she had committed to better. As a result, her efforts were more aligned, more impactful and far more sustainable.

One thing in particular that she said stayed with me:

> Busy had become my identity. But, underneath it, I was overwhelmed and plateauing. Now I ask, 'What do I actually want to achieve today?', 'Why is this important?' and 'How do I want to show up while I do it?'

Through this kind of self-awareness, you can pull yourself out of autopilot and choose intentionality rather than going through the motions. And the way to gain this self-awareness is through knowing your why.

Uncovering your why to harness your most valuable asset

If this idea of the busy trap resonates with you, if you feel like you're constantly rushing but rarely getting the results you want, then it might be time for your own reset.

For each of us, time is our most valuable asset. We all have 24 hours a day and making the best use of this time is not about doing more; it's about doing what matters most — because the future of work won't wait.

Technology is evolving, roles are shifting and industries are transforming. The people who will thrive are those who prioritise their learning and growth, starting now. But to work out exactly what areas you want to prioritise, and which bold moves will provide the most impact for you, you need to uncover your why.

Truth bomb in five whys

One thing I have noticed from working with many women over the years and from watching my friends and family members is that women are very good at prioritising everyone else's needs over their own. We are also not great at asking for help. We don't want to look like we are struggling or not in control of our family, personal lives and careers. The pressure we put on ourselves is crazy!

If you want to succeed in this new era of work, however, you will need to be very intentional about how you spend your time and what matters most to you.

I went through this exact process with a woman — let's call her 'Hannah' — at a workshop I was running. Hannah was a talented senior engineer, and keen to upskill in AI. But, like so many others, she hit me with a familiar line: 'I am so busy at the moment. I just don't have the time.'

So I asked her, 'Why do you want to upskill?'

She replied, 'Because I know how important this is'.

I went a layer deeper: 'Why is it important?'

She said, 'Because that's where all the opportunities will be in the future'.

I asked again, 'Why does that matter to you?'

She responded, 'Because I want to have a thriving career and earn a great income'.

I kept going. 'Why?'

She paused, and then said, 'Because I'm a mum, and I want to be able to support my family'.

One more time, I gently asked, 'And why is that so important to you?'

Her voice softened, 'Because I want to give them a great life full of opportunity'.

I thanked Hannah for her honesty and said, 'This sounds really important to you'. She nodded.

Getting to the root of your motivation, the real reason you want to do something for yourself or others is essential. Without it, you'll always find excuses for not having the time. Through asking why five times, I was able to help Hannah drill down into why upskilling in AI was so important to her.

I responded, 'Then it's going to need to become a priority'.

When something truly matters to you — and you know why it matters — you find the time to focus on it. It's easy to fall into the busy trap or put everyone else's needs above your own. But when you understand why you want something — whether it's learning a new skill, getting promoted or making a career pivot — your intrinsic motivation becomes the driving force.

Knowing your why changes everything.

Boldly applying the five whys in my own life

I did this exercise myself very recently when the idea for this book first came to me. It would have been easy to talk myself out of it; my days and weeks were already full, spent running my recruitment business, podcast, events and mentorship program. I could very easily have said the words, 'I'm just too busy'.

And I won't lie — when the desire first showed up, I shut it down almost immediately. I told myself now wasn't the time, that I'd be stretching myself too thin, and I didn't want to give up my downtime or my weekends.

But the desire and need to write this book began to feel more and more important and urgent every day. I felt it in every:

- call I had with a female candidate talking herself out of a role

- conversation with a hiring manager asking for a new AI skill

(continued)

- mentorship application from a woman feeling stuck and losing hope

- podcast I listened to about the future of work

- workshop where we discussed confidence — or, more often, the lack of it.

The more I had these discussions and experiences, the stronger the urge became and, eventually, the drive to act was louder than the reasons not to.

Knowing this would be one of the most important things I'd ever done and fully aware of the effort and energy it would take, I got crystal clear on why I was writing this book. I knew I had to anchor myself in that purpose, or I'd risk dragging it out, finding endless reasons to pause, or waiting for life to be 'less busy'.

One quiet Sunday afternoon, with a cup of tea beside me and my journal open, I asked myself the following five why questions:

- *Why do you want to write this book?* My answer: 'To give women the confidence, mindset and tools to set themselves up for success and future-proof their careers'.

- *Why is that important?* 'Because the world is speeding up. So many jobs will be obsolete in just a few years, and if women don't have the confidence to upskill, they could get left behind.'

- *Why does that matter?* 'Because I can't live in a world where all the power and decisions are made by one type of person or one gender. Women need to remain in the workforce, not just for their own independence, but to pave the way for future generations.'

- *Why does that matter to me?* 'Because I don't want to see us go backwards. I don't want women to lose their independence and be left with the scraps, doing work that's underpaid and undervalued.'

- *Why does this matter so deeply?* 'Because I've seen what this looks like. I've witnessed firsthand what disempowerment does. I've seen women stuck in situations they can't escape, trapped in loveless or even abusive relationships, because they don't have the financial means or the skills to stand on their own. I've seen women doubt themselves so deeply that they talk themselves out of opportunities before they even try. And I refuse to sit back and watch more women shrink, struggle or settle simply because they didn't have the confidence, clarity or strategies that can make all the difference.'

That is my true why for writing this book. Just thinking about it makes me emotional.

Since doing that exercise for myself, I didn't look back. I wrote consistently, early in the mornings before the sun had even risen, in the quiet of the evenings and, yes, every weekend.

And the best part is — I loved it.

That spark I felt when I connected to my deeper why hasn't faded; it's fuelled me through every chapter of this book, and I hope it's landing with you too. That's been my intention from the very beginning.

Remember — you don't find time, you make it for what matters, and when something truly matters to you, you won't hesitate to protect it. Once you know your why, creating the time becomes the easy part.

So now it's your turn to uncover your why ...

Getting to the bottom of your why

If you've ever said 'I don't have time' to something you know matters to you, this is for you. Instead of lacking time, you're probably lacking clarity. Again, when you deeply understand your why, you stop waiting for time to appear and start making it.

So take advantage of the five whys exercise right now to transform how you connect with your career ambitions.

Grab your notepad, device or journal and complete the following steps:

1. Start with a goal, intention or desire that's important to you. For example:
     (i) 'I want to change careers.'
     (ii) 'I want to start my own business.'
     (iii) 'I want to study AI.'

2. Ask yourself why you want this. Write down the first answer that comes to mind.

3. Then ask why that is important to you to dig deeper. What's behind that first answer?

4. Keep asking 'Why?' three more times. Go deeper — get to the emotion, the purpose and the real reason that this matters to you.

Once you have discovered your true why, write it down and put it somewhere you can see it daily. I like to write my why on a Post-it note and stick it on my laptop so I see it every time I sit down to work.

The next step is turning that inspiration into action and making it a priority. That means no more waiting for the 'perfect moment'. No more squeezing it in around everything else. It's time to schedule it like a meeting, an appointment or a school pick-up.

I have a saying I live by: 'What doesn't get scheduled doesn't get done'. I want you to adopt this into your own life as we move through the remainder of this chapter.

Make your calendar your boss

If I don't set aside time to complete key tasks, I can easily — and have, many times before — find myself floating through the day, unfocused and unsure about where to place my energy.

In the early days of CH Solutions, I didn't understand how important scheduling was. I was incredibly reactive, jumping between emails, candidate calls, meetings and job ads. I never gave myself the space to get into flow. As a result, everything took twice as long as it should. I was exhausted and ineffective. Perhaps this sounds familiar? If so, it's time to get intentional and honest about what steals your precious time.

A great way to explore exactly where you lose time is to try this simple audit. Over the next two to three days, observe and record how you spend your time — and be honest. This is not a judgement exercise; you are just gathering data on what takes your time and energy, and where you could open up space to schedule time to work on what you have identified matters to you.

Once you've gathered your data, ask yourself:

- What time do I wake up?

- What's the first thing I do each morning?

- What time do I start work?

- How many hours do I work?

- What tasks take up the most time?

- How long is my commute?

- How much time do I spend on emails, meetings or social media?

- How do I spend my evenings?

- What time do I go to bed?

- Where do I lose time to distractions or low-value activities?

Once you've written down your responses, review your day more deeply. Where are the time suckers? What's essential? What can be moved, simplified or deleted? What bad habits do you have that you need to add to the 'Stop doing' column in your stop/start list from the previous chapter?

This is such a powerful exercise and one that will build massive self-awareness. Gaining these kinds of insights is also really important before you move on to the chapters in part II, where I help you get really practical on the skills needed in the future of work. The more you can open up space in your calendar, the more prepared you will be for what's next and the skills you will need to begin learning to future-proof your career.

Identify the balls you're juggling

I had a great conversation on the Career Confidence podcast with Tova Angsuwat, former Recruiting Lead at Google. Tova shared a metaphor of juggling multiple balls that perfectly captures the weight of everything we try to balance in our lives, and how much time this takes from us. She broke down the balls we are all trying to juggle into three types, and her description of these types deeply resonated with me.

Here are Tova's three types of balls:

1. *Glass balls:* These are the non-negotiables, and if you drop these balls, they shatter. They include your health, your family, your personal growth, your career development, and the relationships that sustain and stretch you. Neglecting these areas for too long can crack your confidence, stall your momentum and quietly pull you away from the future you want to create. These are the balls to protect.

2. *Bouncy balls*: These are the balls that, if you drop them, will bounce back. They include things like a missed email, the laundry that didn't get done or the text we forgot to reply to — in other words, they're not the end of the world. They can wait, and nothing that truly matters will break if they fall. Take that email you feel you have to answer right away. It might feel urgent but, most of the time, it's not critical. If you don't reply this second, nothing collapses.

The world keeps turning. That's the beauty of a bouncy ball — it hits the floor, but it always comes back up.

3. *Concrete balls:* These are the balls that weigh you down. They include the habits, obligations or even relationships that no longer serve you. If you drop them, honestly, you might feel lighter. These are the balls to consider letting go.

As the following figure highlights, identifying the kinds of balls you're juggling can also help you work out which balls to protect, which ones can wait and which ones can be let go of.

As Tova was describing these balls, I remembered one week in particular when I was racing between tasks, constantly checking my phone, replying to every email the moment it landed, picking up every single call, whether I had the capacity or not. I was juggling so many things, and trying to keep up. I kept telling myself it was all part of being on top of things, responsive and 'professional'. But actually it was simply reactive.

I was giving my best energy to bouncy balls — quick replies, admin tasks and distractions that felt urgent but weren't actually important. I was holding onto concrete balls too, including commitments, habits and even some relationships that were weighing me down more than they were lifting me up.

As I listened to Tova, I remember thinking to myself, *I spend so much time juggling bouncy and concrete balls, and not enough time focusing on my glass balls.* The things that truly mattered — my health, my relationships, my personal growth, my vision for the future — were getting the leftovers. I realised, if I kept living like this, I was going to drop the wrong ball. Something that really mattered was going to crack.

Glass balls
(Protect)

- Health
- Family
- Upskilling
- Personal growth
- Career development
- Meaningful relationships

Bouncy balls
(Can wait)

- Email
- Laundry
- Missed texts
- Non-urgent tasks
- Social media replies
- Minor obligations

Concrete balls
(Let go)

- Old habits
- Outdated obligations
- Relationships that no longer serve you
- Being 'on' outside work hours

The three juggling balls

That was another big wake-up call.

If you are thinking the same thing, ask yourself:

- What are my glass balls?

- What are the bouncy ones I can let fall for now?

- What heavy concrete balls do I need to put down completely?

Too often, we treat everything like a glass ball, and as if the world will fall apart if we don't do it all. But the truth is that some things can wait, some things need protecting and some things, honestly, need letting go.

By this stage of the chapter, I hope you feel motivated and excited to begin prioritising what matters most and allocating your time well — so let's put that awareness to work.

Making use of your newly available time

Now that you've identified where your time could open up and which tasks are important to you, you can now protect this time and these tasks. This is your opportunity to prioritise your future self by putting what is important to you into your schedule, like you would any other non-negotiable.

The following table provides some examples of the kinds of activities you could schedule into your reclaimed time.

Time optimisation table

Time reclaimed	Task time could be used for
Early mornings 30 minutes (before rest of the house wakes up)	Journalling, online courses, reading career books
Commuting 60 minutes (train, bus, walking)	Podcasts, audiobooks, career visioning
Lunch break 30 minutes	Microlearning modules, sending networking messages
Walking the dog 30 minutes	Audio books, podcasts, idea brainstorming
Evenings 30 minutes (post-dinner)	30-minute upskilling sessions, future planning, reading personal development books
TV/scrolling time 60 minutes	Personal growth or reflection
Weekend pocket (1–2 hours)	Learning one skill sprint, online learning, reading

The table provides just a few examples of how you could begin thinking about time allocation, using certain pockets of time more effectively and finding space to upskill.

As shown in the table, one of those slots could be commuting. I love listening to a good podcast or audiobook while commuting, and filling my mind with new ideas or understanding a topic I am curious about in more depth (rather than mindlessly scrolling). I also love stacking good habits on top of each other. For example, when I am moving my body, either at the gym or walking my dog, Ted, I often choose to listen and learn at the same time.

Start by choosing one pocket of time to protect this week. Block it in your calendar. Name it clearly — for example, 'Career power hour', 'AI upskill block', 'Vision planning' or whatever reminds you this time is for you.

Even just 30 minutes a day, used intentionally, can change the entire trajectory of your life and career. Over a year, that's over 180 hours of growth and learning, which can lead to a new opportunity.

How important this is to you and how quickly you want to develop your skills will determine how much time you allocate. My advice is to put in as much effort as you can now, because this will compound and get you prepared for all the change that is coming our way. This is your first act of future-proofing — claiming time for the person and the career you're building and that deserves to be prioritised.

Before we move on to the next part of this book, let me say this loud and clear: you are not selfish for wanting more. You're not wrong to need space for growth, rest, learning, dreaming or anything else.

As women, we've been taught to take care of everyone else first. We show up for the meetings, the family, the group chats and the favours, and then try to squeeze in a bit of time for ourselves if there's anything left. But here's what I know for sure: you can't build a powerful career or exciting future from the scraps of your energy and time. You have to put yourself on your own priority list.

This chapter isn't about hustling harder or adding more to your already full plate. It's about getting honest with yourself about what matters and creating space for that. It's about moving from reacting to life to designing it with intention.

So before you move on, take a second and breathe this in: you're allowed to take up space. You're allowed to prioritise yourself. You're allowed to grow, and you don't need to apologise for it. This is the moment to choose you.

Boldly schedule in time for growth and development

Pull up your calendar on your phone or grab your diary (or whatever you use to track your weeks). Now decide when you are going to schedule time for your own growth and development. You don't need to decide right this second what you will learn during this time (we will spend more time on this in the next part). For now, just block out the time slot and give it a name.

As you do this, watch for any limiting thoughts that pop up, and go back to your true why. Remembering why this is so important to you will be all the motivation you need. Remove any concrete balls you're juggling, and don't get too hung up on the bouncy ones either. Treat this time like a glass ball, one that you do not want to drop, because it may shatter!

The future of work is not waiting for anyone, and if you want to be ready for all the disruptions, upskilling is essential — and that's what we will be diving into next!

From foundation to forward motion

The first part of this book has been all about building your foundation, getting your mindset right, building confidence and creating habits that actually serve you. Without that inner work, none of what comes next will stick. You'll read it, maybe highlight a few things, but you won't do anything with it. I know this because I have not only seen it firsthand with so many people I have coached, but also experienced it myself.

The state of mind we live in daily has the biggest impact on our lives, our choices and how we show up for ourselves and others.

We're in the information age, where everything you need to know is literally at your fingertips. More resources, tools and tactics are available than ever before. And yet, so many people are confused and unsure. According to 2024 research from online platform Glassdoor, 65 per cent of professionals feel stuck in their current careers. That's not a knowledge problem. That's a mindset problem.

This is why we started where we did, because if your head's not in the right place, you won't take the first step, let alone the next one.

But now, you're ready.

In the chapters in the next part, I dive into my strategies for future-proofing your career in a world that's moving at lightning speed. Automation, AI, new industries — it's all changing fast. Those who stay curious, keep learning and choose to act will thrive. The ones who sit still, avoid change or hope things stay the same will be left behind. But you're not here to be left behind.

You're here because you're ambitious, adaptable and ready to take the wheel. You're not waiting to be chosen; you're choosing yourself. This is where things get tactical, and this is where the momentum kicks in.

Let's go.

PART II

CAREER STRATEGIES FOR THRIVING THROUGH CHANGE AND TRANSITION

What you need to do to accelerate your career in the next decade

Chapter 5

Locking in future-proofing skills

The foundations have been laid, now it's time to explore the market demand in more detail and how you can ensure you future-proof your career.

The world of work is undeniably changing at lightning speed. The World Economic Forum's *Future of Jobs Report 2025* reveals that 39 per cent of workers' core skills are projected to shift over the next few years, as rapid technological disruption and evolving business needs continue to redefine the modern workplace. At the same time, global trends such as digitisation, AI and automation are expected to create millions of new jobs. The key to thriving in this environment is future-proofing your skill set: developing a blend of technical abilities and timeless human-centric skills.

While all this change might feel like a lot to take in, here's what I want you to keep front of mind: the future belongs not only to the most technically skilled, but also to the ones who stay open, curious and adaptable. That means you, and now you have the foundations needed to embrace whatever change may come your way. In part I, I shared how courage comes before confidence, the role of fear and how to reframe it, overcoming impostor syndrome and carving out time for what's important. You are well and truly ready to navigate the 'bold gap' and the change coming for all of us!

This chapter is all about giving you the knowledge, tools and confidence to take bold moves. Whether you're early in your career, navigating a pivot, or looking to take the next step in your leadership journey, this is your moment to build a skill set that's both relevant and resilient.

So if you've ever wondered:

- What skills should I be learning right now?

- How do I stay ahead in a changing world?

- What's actually going to help me grow and further my career?

You're in the right place.

Lessons from my live job board

In my home office, I have a whiteboard where I list all the roles I'm currently hiring for. It's how I stay organised but, lately, it's also become a powerful reminder of how much job opportunities are changing. When I look at that board today, I see job titles that didn't exist when I first started in recruitment over a decade ago. Roles like 'machine learning engineer' or 'head of artificial intelligence (AI)' weren't even on the radar back then; now, they're some of the most in-demand positions I'm recruiting for.

The growth in AI-related roles has been exponential. These aren't future jobs, but current ones. Companies aren't just talking about AI anymore. They're hiring for it, and I can say with confidence the roles I'm seeing now are only the beginning. These are just some of the live jobs sitting on my board right now:

- head of AI

- head of risk and compliance

- data scientist

- machine learning engineer

- cybersecurity specialist

- AI engineer

- project manager

- business analyst.

These roles reflect where the world is heading. If you're wondering whether future-proofing your career is worth the effort, this is your sign.

Taking the job brief for the head of AI was a moment. I thought, *Wow! We are now in the future of tech, and it is coming quickly.* What was interesting when taking this job brief from the client was that, yes, the person they wanted for the role needed to have an understanding of technology, but they did not need to come from a strong technical background. What was more important to the hiring manager was what are known as 'human skills'. These were the hiring manager's exact words when they briefed me.

'Georgie, when it comes to technical abilities, I need someone who is about a five. However, when it comes to communication, leadership skills, resilience, adaptability and emotional intelligence, I need someone who is a nine!'

This breakdown really stuck with me. With the rapid rise of AI, the need for someone who's a technical 'gun' isn't as critical as it once was. Many of the 'heavy-lifting' tasks, such as coding, data analytics and automation, can now be done faster and more accurately by machines. What's becoming far more valuable is what AI can't replicate: the ability to adapt quickly, lead teams through uncertainty, think creatively, stay curious, and show up with self-awareness and emotional intelligence. In a world full of tech, it's the deeply human skills that are becoming the real differentiators — and these are what will make you stand out.

I'm going to explore the 'human skills' required to future-proof your career later in this chapter but, for now, let's explore the most in-demand 'hard' skills that companies will be hiring for over this next decade.

Hard skills on the rise

You might be wondering what I mean by 'hard' skills, so let me break it down. Hard skills are the tangible, practical tools in your toolkit. They're the things you can learn, measure, teach and prove. Think of them as the skills you could confidently put on your LinkedIn profile or CV, or talk about in an interview.

Hard skills you currently have might include your ability to write great code, analyse a spreadsheet, run a marketing campaign, build a website, use a CRM or speak a second language. These are the technical, task-based skills that help you do your job.

The thing about hard skills, though, is that they evolve fast. What was considered cutting-edge five years ago might already be outdated. So, staying relevant means checking in regularly and asking yourself, 'Is this skill still in demand?' and 'Am I up to speed?'

And in the age of AI, staying curious and being open to learning is more important than ever.

The World Economic Forum reports that over one billion people will need to upskill over the next five years (and has launched their Reskilling Revolution to help them do so). Roles that didn't even exist a few years ago are now some of the most in-demand jobs across industries.

So, what are some of the roles of the future?

I've done extensive research, read numerous reports, and spoken to my recruitment partners about their workforce plans over the next one to three years, and the skills I cover in this section have repeatedly come up. Note that this could change again over the next 12 months — that's how fast AI and technology are evolving. However, at the time of writing, these are the skills needed for anyone looking to stay relevant in a rapidly changing world.

AI and machine learning

Before I dive into AI, please sit with this for a moment: 'You won't be replaced by AI. You'll be replaced by someone who uses AI'. That line has stuck with me ever since I interviewed Lou Compagnone, director of AI at a major corporation. She stressed, 'AI won't take your job. But the person who knows how to use AI will'.

This perfectly captures where we're at. You don't need to be afraid of AI, but you do need to learn how to work with it, and understand how fast it's moving. We're now seeing the rise of AI agents, tools that can carry out tasks such as booking meetings, replying to emails, analysing reports and even making some decisions. These agents are getting so advanced that some companies are literally adding them into their org charts. Yes, you read that right — AI agents are being assigned roles just like human employees. More than just helping us work, they're also becoming part of the team.

So the real question is: are you ready to work with AI before it starts working around you?

As shown in the following figure, when it comes to working with AI, you have two main options: you either build it or you integrate it. Remember — this is the number one 'hard' skill in the future of work, so opting out is no longer an option.

Let's start with the AI builders. These are those people designing the tools, writing the code, training the data and making the decisions about how AI systems work. Importantly, companies need more women (and minority) builders urgently, because the uncomfortable truth is that bias already exists in AI. We are already seeing tools that favour male candidates, facial recognition that misidentifies women of colour, and algorithms that reinforce outdated stereotypes. That's not the fault of the technology; it's the result of the people who are designing it. If women aren't part of the building process, our perspectives, experiences and realities won't be reflected in the systems shaping the future.

AI builder *Design and create AI systems*	**What you do:** Write code, train data, design AI tools, address bias
	Key roles: Developers, engineers, researchers, product leads
	Skills needed: Technical expertise, programming, system design

AI integrator *Use AI tools to enhance your work*	**What you do:** Apply AI tools, save time, generate ideas, work smarter
	Tools: ChatGPT, Microsoft CoPilot, Google Gemini
	Skills needed: Curiosity, AI literacy, willingness to learn

Will you be an AI builder or an AI integrator?

That's why we need more women in technical roles — such as developers, engineers, researchers and product leads — who are not just consuming AI but shaping it. The more diverse the builders, the fairer and more equitable the AI models will be.

Now, the second bucket: the integrators. This is where most of us sit, and where the opportunity is massive. Again, you don't have to be technical to benefit from AI. But you do have to be curious and open to learning.

Tools such as ChatGPT, Microsoft Copilot and Google Gemini are already changing how we work. Whether you're in recruitment, HR, communication, analysis, marketing, sales, admin — or whatever your role — these tools can help you write smarter, save time, generate ideas and make faster decisions.

I integrate AI daily in my recruitment business. It's helped me write job briefs, research candidates, analyse spreadsheets and write sales messaging. AI not only saves me time, but also helps me be better at my job.

If you're just starting out with integrating AI into your work, keep it simple. Use ChatGPT to write a tricky email. Try Copilot to organise your to-do list. Search YouTube for 'AI in [your job title]' to see what's possible. And, of course, one of the best ways to start is to simply ask ChatGPT — for example, 'How can AI help me save time or work smarter in *[insert your job]*?'

This is exactly how I started — by asking AI questions and taking it one step at a time. The more you use it and review the content it's producing, the more confident you become.

Again, this is the number one skill in demand over the next five years. You don't need to become an AI expert, but you do need to become AI literate.

Over the next decade of work, the people who thrive will be the ones who know how to build with AI or integrate it into how they work. The worst thing you can do is opt out, think it's all too hard, and bury your head in the sand.

One of my standout conversations on the Career Confidence podcast was with Katherine Boiciuc, EY's CTO (chief technical officer). Katherine said something that made me sit up and pay attention. She described AI not as something to fear but as something to see as 'magic'. And, honestly, that shifted something for me.

Instead of feeling like we're all about to be replaced, what if we looked at AI as a tool that could actually boost our creativity and output? Katherine talked about using AI to amplify the skills we already have, not override them. The more we get curious and lean in, the more empowered we become.

Katherine also pointed out something crucial: the biggest gap she sees isn't in access to AI, but in confidence. Most people stop at the mandatory workplace training, but that's just the baseline. To really build confidence and knowledge, we need to go further. And this is where microcredentials come in.

Microcredentials are short, focused courses that help you develop real, practical skills in areas such as generative AI, ethical AI use, prompt engineering or automation tools. Many are free and flexible. These microcredentials are not just about learning; they're also about signalling to yourself and others that you're staying relevant and ready. (I talk more on the importance of this when I explore human skills later in this chapter.) Check out the links to free resources I've included at the end of the book, so you know exactly where to go to begin your AI training.

This is how you go from feeling behind to feeling equipped, from being overwhelmed by change to leading through it. Remember — for women, this matters more than ever. If we don't have a seat at the table in shaping how AI is built and used, then those systems will be created without our perspectives. We'll enter a future coded with bias, reinforcing inequality instead of solving it. By stepping up and learning how AI works, you're future-proofing your career and protecting the future of society.

Data literacy

Data literacy might sound a bit intimidating, but it doesn't need to be. As someone who failed maths in school, if I can start working with data, then trust me, so can you!

Data literacy simply means being able to understand, work with and make decisions based on numbers and information; this is about building confidence with everyday data that helps you do your job better.

Let me give you a real example from my recruitment career. Every week, I look at aspects such as how many roles we've filled, where the best candidates are coming from and how long it's taking us to fill a job vacancy. I track which job ads are performing well, how many people are clicking, how many are actually applying and where we sourced the talent from. This kind of data helps me make smarter decisions, including where to focus my energy or which sourcing strategy to focus on that gets the best results. And these insights from data don't just apply to recruitment.

If you're in marketing, data might show you which posts are driving the most engagement or which email subject lines get the best open rates. If you work in HR, you might be tracking employee retention, pulse survey results or training participation rates. In tech, you might be monitoring website traffic or app usage stats. And if you're a teacher, you could track how many students are completing assignments, or which lessons get the best feedback.

You might not even realise it, but data is everywhere in your day-to-day life. It's how you notice patterns, measure impact and make better choices.

So, where do you start? Open up a dashboard or report you use often and ask yourself, 'What's this actually telling me?' Ask questions like, 'Why is this number higher this week?' or 'Why didn't that campaign land?'

You don't need to become a data expert, but you can look to find the story behind the numbers. Being data literate doesn't mean looking at spreadsheets all day; it means being curious, asking better questions, and using information as a tool to work smarter, not harder.

If understanding data is something you want to explore, I've also provided links to free resources in this area at the end of the book.

Digital literacy

Digital literacy is now a core skill. It's about feeling confident using the tools that help you work smarter, stay organised and communicate effectively. The good news is you're probably already using more digital tools than you realise.

When I'm recruiting, I rely on LinkedIn Recruiter to source candidates, Canva to design ads and my applicant tracking system (ATS) to manage my pipeline. These tools help me move faster, stay on top of tasks, and stay connected to my clients and candidates. Without them, I'd be overwhelmed.

Again, digital literacy isn't just needed in recruitment:

- In marketing, you might be using tools such as Mailchimp, HubSpot or Beehiiv.

- In health care, it could be patient portals and booking systems.

- In admin or operations, you're likely working with CRMs, project trackers or dashboards.

Whether you're managing projects, creating content, scheduling appointments or tracking performance, digital tools are already part of your day-to-day tasks. The difference is how confidently and efficiently you use them.

Like many people, I got thrown into a digital tools crash course during the pandemic. One day we were in the office, and the next we were running meetings on Zoom, chatting on Teams and managing projects on Slack. It showed me how quickly we can adapt when we need to. Once you get comfortable, these tools don't just support your work; they also elevate it.

You don't need to master every platform, but you do need to be open to learning and improving. Digital tools are how work gets done, and the more confident you are with them, the more capable and valuable you become.

As we move away from the Industrial Revolution to the Digital Revolution, every job will include digital tools in some way, so continue to build your competence with them now. Play around with new products to get familiar with how they function so you're always prepared for what's coming next.

Cybersecurity skills

Let's be honest, cybersecurity might not sound like the most exciting skill, but it's one we all need. You don't have to be in IT to understand how to protect your digital identity. If you're online (which we all are), then you're working with sensitive information, and that means you need to know how to keep it safe.

I deal with confidential data every day, including client details, salaries, résumés, contracts and logins. If any of that was leaked or compromised, it would break trust in seconds, and in recruitment (or any people-facing job), trust is everything. That's why I take cybersecurity seriously: to protect the work I do and the people I support.

And I'm not just talking about protecting yourself from the big breaches. You also need to be aware of the small risks — clicking on a fake link, using the same password everywhere or leaving your screen unlocked in a shared space. Those moments add up.

Cyber awareness is now part of being a professional, full stop. And if you're still thinking, *Cyber's not really for me*, let me remind you of Mone, the nurse I introduced in chapter 3 who made a bold pivot into cybersecurity. She had no tech background or coding experience, just a deep desire to keep people safe — not just on the hospital ward but also online. She now works with healthcare organisations to protect sensitive patient data and train staff on how to avoid cyber risks.

Mone's not sitting in a dark room writing code. She's using her people skills, her attention to detail and her calm-in-a-crisis mindset to stop breaches before they happen. She's proof that cybersecurity isn't just for the IT crowd; it's for anyone who wants to protect others, build trust and make an impact in a whole new way.

As of now cyber awareness and security might feel out of reach, but maybe, like Mone, it could be a space where your strengths belong.

So, where do you start with cybersecurity?

You don't need to dive into anything technical right away. Just begin with small, everyday habits. Update your passwords (and don't use the same one everywhere). Turn on two-factor authentication. Be more cautious about clicking unknown links or opening strange emails. All of these actions are already great first steps. Again, this isn't about becoming an expert; it's about protecting yourself, your work and the people who trust you.

If you want to go a little deeper, try a free intro course. I've provided a link to resources at the end of this book. If you want to take it a step further and you're curious like Mone was, look into beginner certifications in cybersecurity.

Project management

Project management might sound a bit corporate but, at the end of the day, it's just about staying organised, moving things forward and actually getting stuff done. Whether you're managing a team, launching something new or simply juggling competing priorities, having this skill is going to set you apart.

You don't need fancy software to be a great project manager. Personally, I rely on Google Sheets, Google Calendar and my

ATS system to keep everything on track. I use Sheets to map out campaigns, track role progress or plan content. Calendar keeps my days structured, keeping track of my interviews, check-ins and deadlines. And my ATS is my hub. It helps me manage talent pipelines, client touchpoints and follow-ups so nothing slips through the cracks.

You're probably managing projects already without even realising it, from hiring timelines to onboarding processes, launching internal initiatives or planning events. In HR, this might be rolling out a new wellbeing initiative. In marketing, it could be prepping a launch. In teaching or admin, it might look like scheduling, reporting or tracking outcomes.

If you want to take things up a notch, you can look into frameworks such as Agile, great if you're working in fast-paced, collaborative environments. But, honestly, just being able to think ahead, communicate clearly and track progress will take you a long way.

In my recruitment career, I have recruited for a number of project managers, and the ones who really stand out don't just manage tasks; they also lead momentum. They can see the big picture, break it down into practical steps and bring the right people together to make it happen. They're equal parts strategist, communicator and problem-solver. If you like to bring order to the chaos, keep things moving and get satisfaction from seeing a plan come to life, then project management is likely already one of your strengths.

If you want to explore more opportunities and how a project manager role could be a good fit, I've again included links to resources offering free courses at the end of this book.

In-demand human skills

Now that we've explored the hard skills companies are focusing on, I hope you feel empowered and enthusiastic about this changing world of work. Let's now talk about something just as important, if not more important: human skills.

These are the things that make us, well … human. They are the skills that can't be automated or outsourced. Abilities such as empathy, communication, curiosity, leadership and critical thinking might not come with a certification or a fancy title, but they're what truly set us apart from machines.

As AI and automation take over more of the technical tasks, these human skills will become your competitive edge. They will help you connect, lead, build trust, navigate change and solve problems.

In the following sections, I unpack the most in-demand human skills, what they look like in the real world, why they matter more than ever and how you can start building them in a way that feels natural.

Analytical thinking

Analytical thinking is all about being able to step back, look at the bigger picture and make smart decisions based on what's really going on. It's about asking better questions, spotting patterns and using what you find to solve problems.

I've really had to work on analytical thinking in my own career. I remember a time when I was recruiting for a senior tech role that just wasn't landing. I'd written what I thought was a strong job ad, pushed it across all the usual platforms, and still … crickets. A few years ago, I might've shrugged it off as a 'tough market' and moved on. But this time, I paused and dug into the data: where I'd posted the ad and the time of day, how many people had viewed it, and how long they stayed on the page.

What I found was that the job title didn't align with what people were searching for. Once I adjusted the title and made the intro more clearly reflect the role's true value, applications started flowing in. Had I not taken that moment to think analytically, I would've missed out on placing a great candidate in a great role.

Analytical thinking is a great skill for everyone to work on. Again, curiosity and asking better questions is a great place to start. Then it's about noticing patterns that others overlook and being willing to explore why something is happening, not just what is happening.

You might already be applying analytical thinking more than you think. It will show up when you pause to reflect on why a meeting landed better than expected or a project stalled. It's there when you adjust your approach based on someone's feedback or test a different way of presenting your ideas. One of the easiest ways to start thinking more analytically is simple to ask 'why' more often:

- Why did that message get more traction?

- Why was that deadline missed?

- Why did this task take longer than usual?

Another helpful habit is to take a moment each week to review one decision you made, big or small, and ask yourself what information you used to make it, what assumptions you were working with and how things played out. This reflection helps you spot patterns and sharpen your instincts over time.

Even experimenting in small ways can strengthen this skill. For example, try two different approaches to the same task and compare the results. Notice what changed and why. When you look at a report or a set of results, challenge yourself to explain the story behind the numbers in just a sentence or two. When something goes really well, don't just celebrate it, analyse it. Ask yourself:

- What made it successful?

- Was it timing?

- Was it the way I framed it?

The goal is to move from 'that worked' to 'that worked because ...'

Analytical thinking is about staying curious, asking sharper questions, and being willing to pause and look twice when most people are already moving on.

Creative thinking

You may think creative thinking is for the 'arty' types and, to be honest, I used to think the same thing. I had a limiting story that told me I wasn't the creative type. But this line of thinking could get you and me in trouble, so it's time to reframe this.

You'll see creative thinking pop up in all kinds of roles and, no, it's not about being the most 'out there' person in the room. It's about being the one who sees a better way and gives it a go.

In tech, the creative thinker might be the developer who figures out a quicker way to ship a feature or automates something that's been done manually for years. Thinking creatively is about improving the process, not just following it.

In marketing, it could be someone who turns a long, boring update into a scroll-stopping story or tests a new way to connect with the audience — for example, jumping on a trend or using video when everyone else is still sending PDFs.

In teaching, it might be switching up the way content is delivered, perhaps using a game instead of a worksheet, or a project or real-life example that lands with students.

In leadership, thinking creatively is all about finding better ways to motivate your team. Maybe it's the way you run one-on-ones, or how you celebrate wins, finding something that feels more human and less 'tick-the-box'.

For me, creative thinking has provided a huge advantage in the way I approach recruitment. Instead of just blasting the database or posting another generic job ad, I have applied creative thinking to come up with new ways of attracting top talent. I have sent voice notes through LinkedIn messenger to create trust and traction with top talent. I utilise the Career Confidence podcast and create ads for new jobs, I set up marketing campaigns using our CMS systems, I have joined online groups and attended networking events in the attempt to try something different and find a better way of getting to the end result.

If you want to improve your creative thinking, start by paying attention to the things in your day that feel a bit frustrating or just unnecessarily hard. That 'ugh, surely there's a better way to do this' feeling is your cue to try something new!

You don't have to try anything big at first. Start with just a small tweak. Rewrite a clunky email. Try a fresh way of running a meeting. Use ChatGPT to help you brainstorm instead of staring at a blank page. The more you train yourself to think this way, the easier it will become.

Resilience, flexibility and adaptability

I devoted a lot of chapter 3 to resilience and adaptability because, honestly, it shows up everywhere. In a world that's constantly shifting, the ability to bounce back, adapt quickly and stay grounded through change is one of the most important skills you can build.

As outlined in chapter 3, resilience isn't about pushing through; it's about learning from the tough stuff and working through the ongoing challenges that come your way, without letting them take you on a spiral. Flexibility is about staying open when plans shift (because they will). And adaptability is being able to pivot without panicking when something unexpected lands in your lap, such as a new tool, a restructure or a change in direction.

I've experienced the unexpected firsthand in recruitment: roles suddenly get pulled, hiring freezes happen and priorities shift overnight. I've had to learn to move with it, not without frustration, I'll be honest, but with a mindset that says, 'All right, let's figure this out'.

And this need for resilience, flexibility and adaptability applies across the board, in every industry. For example, in leadership, these human skills help you to steer your team through change without burning out. In marketing, they help you adjust your whole campaign when the algorithm changes (again). These skills are a constant work in progress and a muscle I continue to build. I catch myself beginning to react when things don't go to plan, and for a control freak like me, that can be tough. I give myself a moment and then ask, 'What can I control here?' If I begin to feel myself getting stressed or anxious, I do the control test, and ensure I am not focusing on all the things that I have no power to influence — which, in truth, is most things.

I can't control whether a client decides to pull the pin on a role I have spent hours headhunting for, I can't control whether a new marketing campaign bombs, I can't control how a candidate performs in an interview, and I can't control a lot of external factors. However, I can control how I respond to the situation in front of me. It has taken a long time for me to understand and fully put this concept into practice, and some days are easier than others, which is why it continues to be a work in progress. The more I practise this, the easier it becomes to stay steady when everything around me is shifting.

So next time something doesn't go to plan, big or small, take a breath and do a quick 'control scan'. What's actually within your power to change or influence right now? What's not?

Write it down if it helps. The more you practise this, the faster you'll bounce back next time life throws a curveball.

The bottom line here is that we are entering a time where change is going to be the only constant, and those of us who continue to work on ourselves and these core skills will be the ones who go on to thrive over this next decade of work.

Empathy and active listening

Empathy and listening are human skills at their core. They build trust and deepen relationships.

I used to think being a good listener meant staying quiet while someone else talked. But active listening is a whole other level. It's about being fully present, not thinking about your response, but truly tuning in to what someone is saying (and often what they're not saying). It means picking up on tone, body language, hesitation and emotion. When you listen actively, people feel seen, safe and respected. I honestly believe in this hyper-technical digital age, in which so many seem glued to screens, the biggest gift you can give someone is your full attention.

Empathy builds on that. It's not about fixing someone's problem or pretending to know exactly how they feel; it's about genuinely trying to understand their perspective. It's saying, 'I hear you', and really meaning it. You might not agree with them, and that's okay. That's what makes us different. If we all thought the same, looked the same and had the same ideas and perspectives, the world would be a pretty dull place. Our uniqueness makes us human. When it comes to empathy, the point is to connect with others' long enough to see the world through their eyes, even if just for a moment.

In my career, the moments when I've built the strongest relationships haven't come from what I've said but from how I've listened. I've learned that when someone feels heard, they're more open to feedback, more willing to collaborate and more likely to trust you when things get tough.

I have been thinking about these skills a lot and have realised that empathy and active listening will become even more critical as the future of work evolves. We're already working across cultures and time zones, and, for the first time, up to five generations are sharing the same workplace. That means vastly different life experiences, value systems and ways of working, often under the same roof.

Add to that the increasing importance of inclusion across gender, race, neurodiversity and lived experience, and it's clear: a one-size-fits-all approach to communication doesn't cut it anymore. What lands well with one person might completely miss the mark with another. A joke that feels harmless to you might feel isolating or offensive to someone else. Even feedback can land differently depending on how someone was raised or what they've experienced in the past.

Empathy allows you to navigate this complexity with respect. It helps you pause and consider, 'How might this land for them?' Active listening helps you check your assumptions before you act. It gives you the opportunity to notice when something's off and open a conversation rather than shutting one down.

These skills aren't just about being polite or nice; they're about being effective, especially in environments that are more diverse and distributed than ever before.

Curiosity and lifelong learning

I remember reading that 'curiosity' was one of the most in-demand skills for the future of work and, honestly, it made me smile. For a long time, curiosity didn't get much credit. At school, you were rewarded for having the right answer, not asking the better question. But in today's world, and especially in the one we're stepping into, curiosity is the thing that will keep you relevant.

Lifelong learning isn't just a nice idea anymore, either. Entire industries are evolving at a pace, and the traditional education system wasn't designed for it. That system was built for the Industrial Revolution, where the goal was to train people for predictable jobs on structured paths. But we're now in the Digital Revolution, where change is constant and roles are being reinvented all the time. Our education system simply hasn't caught up — it's still too slow, too rigid and too far removed from the real skills people need today.

We can't afford to wait for institutions to figure it out. We have to take ownership of our own learning journeys — and that's where curiosity comes in. You need to start asking, 'What don't I know yet?' or 'What else is possible here?' Questions like these get you exploring, experimenting and updating your skill set, not every five years, but every few months!

This is where microlearning and microcredentials come into play. You don't need a new degree to stay relevant, but you do need to set aside time to invest in your growth — whether that's listening to a podcast on your walk, completing a short online course, or reading an article that gets you thinking. These bite-sized moments of growth add up, and they matter far more than any one certificate or degree ever could.

One observation I have made in over a decade working in recruitment is that the career professionals who grow the fastest aren't the ones with the fanciest qualifications. In fact, I couldn't even tell you the last time I was asked for someone with a degree.

The people who get ahead and succeed are the ones who practise all the human skills I have shared. They don't wait for the perfect time before they start something or decide to learn a new skill; they just start, and that mindset compounds into real capability and real confidence.

If you're unsure where to begin when it comes to learning, it's time to get curious and do a career skills audit. (The following exercise outlines how.) This is something I encourage you to do often because, in the future of work, learning is no longer a one-off event; it's a habit that you will need to do often and as new tools and opportunities arise.

Complete a career skills audit and own your next bold move

All right, let's bring it all together. You've just explored the five 'hard' and the five 'human' skills shaping the future of work; now it's time to apply the insights to your own career. This is where self-awareness comes in. Think of this exercise as your personal career audit, giving you a chance to zoom out, take stock and ask:

- What do I already bring to the table?

- What gaps do I want to close?

- Where do I want to grow next?

This isn't about panic-learning everything on the list or becoming a master of AI overnight. It's about tuning into what's relevant for you, including your goals, your values and your future. Because, as you know, building confidence doesn't come from having it all figured out. It comes from making a bold decision and having the courage to take the next step, and then showing up for it.

(continued)

117

Using your journal, device or a notepad, think about and jot down some responses to the following:

- Make a list of the skills included in this chapter. Circle the ones that excite you and the ones you already have, and then put a question mark next to the ones that feel like a stretch.

- Make a separate list of the skills you've circled and keep this list close. In the next chapter, I help you explore how your current skills can transition into new roles, promotions and industries. You will need to be open-minded, curious and adaptable to this, but remember — you have everything you need to succeed. Let me show you how.

Chapter 6

Pivoting with clarity and confidence

areer transitions used to be the exception; now, they're becoming the expectation. According to recent research by international recruitment agency Kingsley, 59 per cent of today's workforce will need to upskill or re-skill over the next five years just to stay relevant. The pace of change, driven by AI, automation and evolving business needs, means more people will need to shift direction, rethink their strengths and pivot into new spaces.

The good news is you don't need to start from scratch. You already have skills, experiences and insights that matter. The key is knowing how to spot them and how to apply them in new and relevant ways.

In this chapter, I unpack how to pivot in your career with clarity and confidence. Whether you're changing roles or industries, going for a promotion or simply future-proofing where you are now, it's about making the shift with intention rather than panic.

Let's break it down.

Stuck to unstoppable

If you're mid-career and feeling stuck in a role that no longer fits, you're not alone. The idea that we have one career for life is long gone. In fact, 2023 research from career planning website Zippia.com shows that the average age for a significant career change is 39. Shifting gears in your 30s, 40s and 50s is now more common than ever.

Aiming for the perfect linear career path is no longer realistic; instead, your focus needs to be on knowing how to bring your core skills, both hard and human, into new contexts. Speaking with multiple hiring managers each week, I can assure you that employers are not looking for tech geniuses. They want people who can think critically, problem-solve, and lead with empathy and fresh perspectives.

Businesses and emerging industries need what *you* bring to the table. Your job now is to package those skills with purpose, position yourself for what's next, and take bold, intentional steps forward. Whether you're looking to pivot out into a completely new industry, step into a different role in the company you are working for now, or finally go for that next-level promotion, you are about to learn how to use what you already have to move with clarity and confidence. So, where do you start?

The good news is that you have already begun the inner work. You've also explored the future of work and the skills that are rising and in demand, from AI and data literacy to resilience and adaptability. Now it's time to make your move, in whatever direction you choose. Career pivots are happening every day. And the people making them aren't the most qualified on paper. They're the ones who know how to back themselves, leverage what they've got, and take intentional steps forward.

This is where my BOLD pivoting formula comes in.

Embracing change with the BOLD pivoting formula

Career change doesn't have to be overwhelming. You don't need to have it all figured out; you just need a place to begin.

The BOLD pivoting formula breaks your pivot down into four clear, empowering steps:

1. *Begin where you are:* Start by focusing on what you're already good at. You've built years of experience, and now it's time to unpack those transferable skills, passions and superpowers that can be applied in a whole new way.

2. *Open opportunities to you:* Explore what's possible. Look at growing industries, future-focused roles and where your existing strengths might shine in a new context, especially in tech, digital and emerging fields.

3. *Learn what you need:* Identify the gaps. Whether this is learning about new tools, gaining certifications, or simply increasing your industry knowledge, you don't need to become an expert overnight; you just need to start learning intentionally and strategically.

4. ***Do the work:*** Bold moves require bold action. Take small steps. Reach out, apply, build, test and iterate. The clarity and confidence you're craving will not come from thinking but from doing.

In the following sections, I walk you through each step of the BOLD pivoting formula. My goal is to give you something real and practical to lean on as you decide what to do or where to move next.

Begin where you are

You don't need to have it all figured out to take the first step. You need to pause, look inward and start with what you already have: the skills, strengths and experiences you've built over time.

As you think about where you are now, remember to keep one important aspect front of mind — something that has shown up repeatedly in my conversations with thousands of career professionals over the past decade of my recruitment career. The biggest barrier to making a career transition is rarely skill-based. It's mental and emotional, based on the fear of getting it wrong, of what others will think, of being too late or too old, and of the unknown. If you want to future-proof your career and stay ahead in this next decade of work, you can't afford to think like this. If you still doubt your abilities or are fearful, read over the first part of this book again. Go back to your why. Ground yourself and remember — first you must have courage, and then the confidence will catch up.

You've done more than you likely give yourself credit for. Whether you've been managing teams, juggling deadlines, caring for others, solving problems or keeping things running behind the scenes, those moments have shaped you. They've taught you how to lead, adapt, problem-solve, communicate and think on your feet. These are the fundamental skills employers seek, and they're already yours. This is the perspective shift I want you to adopt moving forward, because you are not starting from scratch; you're starting with wisdom and a tonne of experience.

We all have transferable skills. These skills travel with you, wherever you want to go, and they are your assets in this new world of work. However, not all strengths and skills travel equally. Some will be more in demand than others. Some you may need to leave behind, and others you will need to double down on — especially skills like adaptability, clear communication and the ability to work with AI. Others might belong to an older version of your career and may no longer serve where you're heading next. And that's okay.

Imagine for a moment you're packing for a one-way flight to your future career.

You've got a suitcase, a 20-kilogram baggage limit and no option to bring your whole wardrobe. Some clothes no longer fit or are dated, so they aren't getting packed. You are only taking with you the clothes you love to wear, that you feel confident in, that make you stand out — and that are suited to your destination. So, what are you packing?

Now let's relate this to your career.

- What strengths are essential for where you want to go?

- What skills do you want to leave behind?

- What might need a little upgrade before it earns a spot in your suitcase?

This is about being intentional and doubling down on what energises you and sets you up for growth in a changing world of work.

Take a moment, and in your journal or notepad or on your device create two columns. At the top of the first, write 'Hard skills I'm taking with me'; at the top of the other, write 'Human skills I'm taking with me.'

As you start filling out each column, ensure you think about the skills that will be in demand in the future. For example, if one of your hard skills is digital literacy and you are well-versed in using platforms such as Canva, Microsoft Teams, Slack, Adobe or Xero, these skills would be valuable because they are used across multiple businesses and industries. So make sure you include them.

You may also find yourself playing around with AI tools and becoming more AI-literate, building skills in partnering with tools such as ChatGPT, Microsoft Copilot or Google Gemini in your day-to-day work. As discussed, these skills are already showing up across every industry, and so should definitely get packed!

Once you have listed all the 'hard skills' you are taking with you, move on to your human skills. Sure, AI can write code and answer questions, but it can't lead with empathy, hold space for someone struggling, or influence a room with clarity and care. That's where these human skills come in — so what's getting packed for you?

For example, are you steady in uncertainty, bounce back after setbacks and move with change instead of resisting it? This is what adaptability and resilience look like and, as already covered in detail, will be a huge advantage as the world of work speeds up. Can you clearly share ideas, tell stories and bring people with you?

In hybrid teams, cross-functional roles and global organisations, clear, confident communication is everything.

If you have these human skills, make sure you include them on your list!

The following table provides some further examples of what you might be able to include on your 'packing' list as you prepare for a career pivot.

Potential hard and human skills to pack during a career pivot

Hard skills I'm taking with me	Human skills I'm taking with me
Canva (content creation and design)	Empathy
Microsoft Excel/PowerPoint/ Outlook	Active listening
Xero (or other accounting software)	Emotional intelligence
CRM systems (e.g. HubSpot, Salesforce)	Adaptability
Project management tools (e.g. Trello, Asana)	Problem-solving
Social media platforms (e.g. LinkedIn, Instagram)	Creative thinking

Once you have written down all your hard and human skills, take a moment and give yourself huge credit for the skills you've built. This is such a powerful exercise and one that will set you up for what's next.

If you are looking at your list concerned that you're not packing much, don't panic; that's also great awareness. For now, begin and accept where you are, because awareness is the first and most powerful step towards change.

Open opportunities to you

You've packed your suitcase. You know what strengths, skills and experiences you're bringing with you in your career pivot — the ones that energise you, and are in demand for the future of work. Now it's time to look ahead and start exploring what's out there.

This part of the journey is like flipping through a travel brochure, but instead of considering Bali or Barcelona, you're looking at career destinations, and roles, industries and opportunities that match your skill set and stretch your potential.

Some will feel familiar, and others will feel exciting, maybe even a little uncomfortable, and that's okay. Remember — fear is not a red flag; it's a signal that you are growing and stepping into the unknown. You're not committing to one direction just yet; you're simply getting curious, exploring the map and seeing what's possible. And don't forget — a pivot doesn't always mean changing industries or starting something on the side. Sometimes, a 'pivot' might mean stepping up into a promotion, a leadership role or a new challenge within the path you're already on. A pivot can look like anything that stretches you.

Here's how to start exploring:

1. Start by searching job ads like a researcher, not a job seeker.

2. Jump onto platforms such as Seek, Indeed or LinkedIn Jobs, but don't type in the job title you've always had; type

in a skill or strength you want to use more of. For example, 'customer experience', 'project management', 'stakeholder engagement', 'user research', 'AI tools', 'sales' or even 'problem-solving'. See what comes up.

3. What roles are asking for the things you already know how to do? Make a note of:
   - roles or titles that come up often
   - skills they're asking for that you already have
   - anything you're missing (so you can upskill with purpose).

   At this stage, you're not trying to find a job. You're simply researching how your strengths show up across different industries and careers. And, trust me, they do.

4. Next, talk to people doing work that piques your interest.

Once you have gathered some information from the job boards, it's time to use those insights intentionally, because the best perspectives will come from real conversations. If you have a friend or a friend of a friend or a family member who is currently working in a job or industry you want to explore, reach out to them. This is where you get super curious and ask questions. People love to talk about their roles and, in my experience, are always happy to help.

If you don't have anyone in your network, start looking to connect with people on LinkedIn. You could begin by typing a skill or job title into the search bar and see who is in your current location or who you are already connected to. For example, you could type 'data analyst' in the search bar, followed by your location. This will bring up a good list of professionals.

This is also great research, because you can see their backgrounds, the types of companies they work for and the jobs they have had previously. In this way, checking LinkedIn profiles is like looking into people's online résumés, giving you more insights when considering your next move.

You could also search for career coaches or recruitment agencies specialising in certain industries you want to explore. Ask for advice on the market and what's happening in the space. Having as many conversations as you can is key.

If you are reaching out to people on LinkedIn whom you have never met, make sure you customise the message, and keep it short, warm and focused on shared interest, not a sales pitch. Here's a simple template:

> Hi [name], *I came across your profile while exploring roles in* [industry/field] *and I'd love to learn more about what you do. I'm currently exploring a career pivot, and your path really stood out to me. Would you be open to a quick chat or sharing a bit about your journey?*
>
> [Your name]

(I discuss the importance of your LinkedIn profile in the next chapter and provide tips on how to set it up for success, because this will impact the number of people who accept your connection request.)

Once you have a virtual or in-person coffee chat locked in with someone you know or someone new, make sure you go prepared with some questions. A great place to start is by asking them, 'What do you do on a day-to-day basis?' This will open up a great dialogue and give you a great peek into what their job looks like, and whether this aligns with your skills and values.

Some other great questions to help you dive deeper include the following:

- *What do you love most about your work?* (This helps you tune into what could feel energising for you.)

- *What skills do you rely on most in your day-to-day work?* (This helps you match what you already have.)

- *Which part of your job feels the most rewarding? Which part feels the hardest?* (This helps you to assess alignment with your own energy and strengths.)

- *What does success look like in your role?* (This helps you to check if that feels aligned with your goals.)

- *What kind of person thrives in this role or industry?* (A good one for checking if your strengths or values are a fit.)

- *If someone with my background wanted to pivot into your space, what would you recommend they do first?* (This helps you get tactical, not just inspired.)

Go into these conversations with a curious and open mind. The more insights and information you can gather, the more clarity you will gain, making it easier to make your next bold move.

Once you have a clear idea of your transferable skills and how they match current market opportunities, it's time for the next step in the BOLD pivoting formula.

Learn what you need

You've done the work. You've reflected, packed your suitcase with strengths and skills, and explored where those could take you next. Now it's time to get real about what might be missing in your skill set and learn what's needed to take that next bold step. This is not about doing tonnes of study or mastering everything overnight. This is about choosing to grow with intention and making yourself a priority.

Learning is your bridge to moving from where you are now to where you want to be without overwhelm. This is where you begin to spot the gaps and understand what's missing.

Look at the job ads, and think about the insights from all your conversations and roles that caught your eye. What skills came up that you don't have or feel confident in yet? I want to pause here for a moment, because the word *yet* is very powerful here. Saying, 'I'm not confident with that … *yet*' keeps you open. It reminds you that growth is possible. Just because you haven't done something before doesn't mean you can't figure it out. This simple word shifts your mindset from 'I can't' to 'I'm on the way'.

Now ask yourself:

- What keeps showing up that you've never done, but could learn?

- What human skills, such as leadership, influence or communication, do you know you need to strengthen?

- What's going to build your confidence the most right now?

For example, you might see 'experience with CRMs', 'using AI tools', or 'data-driven decision making' coming up a lot.

Once you've identified your gaps, choose *one* skill to focus on. Please don't try to learn everything all at once; that's the fastest road I know to overwhelm. Pick one skill to focus on — one that excites you or will stretch you a little (in a good way), or one that feels like it would give you more confidence in your day-to-day role.

I call this mini learning challenge a 'one-skill sprint'. For example, you may decide to expand your knowledge with AI tools. Rather than overthinking or complicating this, you could simply prompt ChatGPT with the following:

Act as my personal AI coach. Create a simple, seven-day beginner plan to build my AI literacy, with one 30-minute action per day. Make it hands-on, no fluff, and help me feel more confident using AI in my work.

This is a great place to start, because you're also using AI immediately, which will build competence and confidence.

Alternatively, you may decide to learn more about effective communication, because you have identified that not being skilled in this area could hold you back as you step into a leadership role. Define what good, clear communication means to you, and then schedule in learning time. This could mean choosing an online course, or recording yourself speaking about a topic and listening back to how you sound. Or it could look like listening to podcasts and YouTube videos with experts speaking on the topic, or even being really brave and enrolling in a public speaking class.

Remember that curiosity and continuous learning are core skills needed in the future of work, meaning you will never reach the finish line when it comes to upskilling and re-skilling, especially if you want to stay relevant. So pick one thing to work on and focus on that until you feel improvements have been made and you begin to feel more confident with that future skill.

Do the work

The final step in the BOLD pivoting formula is the most important. I have seen people spend hours, weeks and months thinking about what to do, but never actually taking the next step and doing the work!

Your career is your responsibility, and if you don't take this final step, all the planning, reading and research will be in vain. This doesn't mean hustling every hour or burning yourself out trying to learn everything. It means showing up and taking consistent action, even if it's hard, even if you feel like you're figuring it out as you go (because you are).

On some days, the couch and Netflix will feel more tempting than finishing that AI course. You'll have mornings when hitting snooze wins over updating your CV, moments when scrolling feels safer than reaching out to someone new on LinkedIn, and weeks when life gets busy and your learning plan quietly slips to the bottom of the list. And at certain points impostor syndrome will no doubt creep in and make you question whether you've really got what it takes. That's all normal. But these are the exact moments that count — the forks in the road where you either choose comfort or growth. You don't have to get it right every time. You just have to keep choosing to show up more often than you don't.

Boldly pivoting from beauty therapist to technology recruitment consultant

Now that you know the BOLD pivoting formula, you're probably starting to connect the dots in your own journey, and that's exactly the point. Before you dive into mapping out your next move, I want to share a story of what a bold career pivot looks like in real life.

Here's how I went from beauty therapist to technology recruitment consultant, and how each step of the BOLD pivoting framework showed up along the way.

I'll be honest — I couldn't wait to leave school. Even though I got good grades, I craved adventure. At 16, I left to study beauty therapy in Oxford, aiming to work on cruise ships and see the world. But first, I needed real experience. So I secured a role managing a spa on a luxury estate in the Cotswolds, learning the ropes of customer service, sales and marketing.

Cruise ships lost their appeal after I had an in-depth chat with someone who worked on them (the power of conversations), and I realised seasickness and months at sea weren't for me. Instead, I joined Mark Warner, a UK-based travel company and flew to Greece during the summer months and to the French Alps in the winter to help run their resort spas.

Every week brought new guests and fresh targets and I soon learned how to negotiate, sell and lead. I consistently hit my targets through creative thinking and coming up with new promotions to get bookings.

After two incredible years in Europe, I returned to the United Kingdom briefly, but I had my sights set on Australia.

(continued)

During my time working for Mark Warner, I'd built resilience and adaptability, and given myself the proof that I could start again from anywhere. So, when I arrived in Melbourne, I was able to land a job fast. After six months running a clinic, I realised I wanted to make Australia home; however, in order to stay, I needed sponsorship. That's when I realised I was going to have to make a bold move.

Applying the BOLD pivoting formula, I started at the beginning, with my current level of skills and experience. I began identifying a number of strengths:

- Firstly, I was great with people. I had met so many individuals from all walks of life in my six years as a therapist, and had always been able to build rapport quickly, making them feel comfortable, seen and valued.

- Secondly, I was great at sales, even before I realised it. Every role I'd had had come with targets, and I consistently exceeded them — for example, through upselling products and packages, or offering new treatments. I guess I never felt like I was 'selling', because I genuinely believed in what I was offering, and that belief made it easy to connect with people and help them choose what was right for them.

- Thirdly, I picked up technology quickly. Every spa or clinic I worked for had a new booking system to manage and a client database to navigate, which I would always pick up with ease.

- Last but not least, I had a number of human skills, such as active listening, resilience, problem-solving and emotional intelligence. These were all my foundations. Now, I just needed to repackage them and transfer them to a new industry, and that's exactly what I did.

Taking stock of the skills you already have is so powerful. It gives you clarity, confidence and certainty that you have what it takes to make the bold move. No matter what industry or career you are in at present, you do have meaningful and transferable skills that businesses are crying out for.

When I was working as a beauty therapist, I never imagined I'd one day be running my own technology recruitment company but, as you can see, I didn't leave all my experience behind. I brought it with me. The way I connected with clients, built trust quickly, listened deeply and genuinely cared translated. I just had to learn how to position those strengths differently.

When I decided to career pivot and had identified what my strengths and transferable skills were, I began the next step of the BOLD pivoting formula by researching opportunities and checking out job ad sites such as Seek and Indeed. I remember feeling excited but slightly overwhelmed when I did this myself.

I didn't type in 'recruitment consultant' because I had no idea this job would fit my current skill set. I knew I was good at sales and customer service, so that's exactly what I typed into the job boards. A whole new world of opportunities opened up, and that's where I saw the ad for a 'junior recruitment consultant'.

As I scanned the job brief, I asked myself:

- What skills or qualities are showing up again and again?

- Which of these do I already have?

- What would I need to learn or strengthen?

(continued)

I began noting the pattern and realised I ticked more boxes than I first thought, especially regarding communication, problem-solving, sales and customer experience.

Before I hit apply, I made sure the keywords from the job ad were reflected in my CV. This step really matters, especially now, with most companies using ATS to scan and filter applications. If your résumé doesn't include the language companies are looking for, it might not even reach a real person. That's why I always recommend tailoring your CV to the job ad as much as possible. It's a small shift that can make a big difference in getting noticed. I decided I had nothing to lose, so I picked a job, uploaded my CV and hit reply.

A few days went past, and I had heard nothing. Instead of sitting around waiting, I decided to take action. The ad had a number, so I decided to pick up my phone and call. A man, let's call him Tom, answered, and I knew I didn't have long to get his attention, so I quickly introduced myself, explained that I had applied for the junior recruitment consultant role, and outlined why I was an excellent fit for the position. At no point did I feel confident doing this, but I knew if I wanted to get a new job in a new industry, I had to do whatever it took to make it happen. After a few minutes of me talking (probably way too fast, and without coming up for air), he offered me the opportunity to come in for an interview. I was delighted! Tom later told me that he had massive respect for me calling him, and thought it said a lot about my character, which would prove to be a big contributor to my success in recruitment.

The day of the interview came. I didn't have LinkedIn back then, so I couldn't do what I would do now and look up the hiring manager and team online before the interview. I did as much research as I could, bought myself a new smart dress to wear and headed for the interview. When I arrived at the reception area, ten others were in the waiting room. I remember feeling really nervous and concerned. Looking around the room, there seemed to be some well-presented and smart people there. Looking back now, I realise I had massive impostor syndrome.

After a few minutes of waiting, two men in sharp suits walked in and asked all of us to come through together. I remember thinking, *Wait... isn't this supposed to be a one-on-one interview?* Clearly, I was wrong.

We were there for over three hours. It turned out to be a group assessment, and we had to complete a series of exercises. The one that really stuck with me was a role play. Tom (the person who had originally invited me in) played the part of a frustrated client, and my job was to calm him down.

Thankfully, I'd had plenty of experience with tricky clients while managing spas, so this wasn't new. I listened carefully, let him speak, acknowledged what he was feeling, and made sure he felt heard and respected. Then I calmly offered a solution and talked through the next steps I'd take.

When Tom hung up the phone and broke character, he looked at me and said, 'Georgie, that was great. Where did you learn how to handle challenging clients like that?'

This is an example of what transferable skills can look like. Something that came easily to me, because of my previous experience dealing with customers, was now a much-needed skill in the industry I wanted to pivot into.

A week later, I got the call: I'd landed the job. But here's the part I really want you to sit with: some people in that room were, on paper, far more qualified than me. Some had degrees, while others had already worked in HR or recruitment.

(continued)

But those qualifications and experience weren't what sealed the deal. The hiring manager wasn't just looking for someone who ticked every box on a résumé. They were looking for strong human skills, such as emotional intelligence, critical thinking, problem-solving and leadership potential. Those were my strengths. And I made sure they saw them.

The next six months were a steep learning curve, as the 'L' in the BOLD pivoting formula truly kicked in. I had so much to learn, and some days I definitely questioned whether I'd ever get my head around all the tech jargon on a CV, ask the right qualifying questions or confidently present top talent to clients. It was a lot. But the strong foundation I'd built as a therapist, especially my people and digital skills, helped me pick things up quickly. I threw myself into learning: reading every blog and article I could find on recruitment, and shadowing some of the top consultants in the office. I've always believed that most things are caught, not taught; we learn by watching what works and putting it into practice.

This is where the 'D' in the BOLD pivoting formula comes in — don't read or plan; do. Most people get stuck at this point, because doing means putting yourself out there before you feel ready. For me, this looked like fumbling through my first few calls, rewriting my outreach emails ten times and showing up to meetings where I felt out of my depth. But that's exactly what I did. I made the call. I booked the meeting. I asked the questions consistently, even when I wasn't sure I was asking the 'right' ones. I didn't wait for confidence. I built it by doing the reps, because progress didn't come from thinking about it. It came from action, one foot in front of the other, one bold move at a time.

Pivoting up in leadership

Even if you're not switching industries entirely, the same rules apply when you're aiming for a promotion. You still need to take stock of your strengths and skills, because that's where your confidence to step up starts. You also need to look for opportunities, and consider where this next move will lead, and whether it is setting you up for success in the future of work.

Learning new skills is part of the deal if you want to move up. What got you to where you are won't get you to where you want to be. You'll have to do the work, even when it feels uncomfortable. That might mean asking for more responsibility before you're given the title, negotiating a raise or benefits that actually align with your values, or speaking up in rooms you used to shrink back from. Promotions don't just happen; they follow a bold formula. (I discuss pivoting up and negotiation in more detail in chapter 8.)

Plan your bold career pivot

Now it's your turn. You've just seen what it looks like to put the BOLD pivoting formula into action. You've worked out your strengths, explored new possible opportunities, identified skill gaps, and hopefully felt a flicker of excitement about what your next chapter could be.

This is your moment to take stock. Let's begin bringing it all together. Grab your journal, device or notepad, and get ready to plan your BOLD career pivot.

(continued)

Step 1: Revisit your suitcase

Look at your list of everything you're bringing with you, both human and hard skills, which you created earlier in this chapter. Ask yourself:

- What's in there that you're proud of?

- What's most valuable in today's market?

- What might need to be left behind?

Next, ask yourself:

- What are you already good at that aligns with the future of work?

- Which strengths do you want to lean into more?

- What part of your experience do you tend to overlook or undervalue?

Step 2: Reimagine your destination

Now that you know what you're carrying, it's time to zoom out and explore where those skills could take you. But instead of looking for the job, look for the match where your skills, values and interests intersect.

Try this:

1. Type one of your top skills into a job site (such as Seek or LinkedIn) and see what titles come up.

2. Jot down three to five roles that spark curiosity, even if they feel like a stretch.

3. Message one person in that space. If you know them, great; if not, type the job title into LinkedIn to find

some options. Reach out to at least ten people a week. Be sure to customise the message (refer to earlier in this chapter for an example).

4. Ask for a quick call or offer to buy them coffee if they have time. Go prepared with questions to ask and be open and curious to whatever they have to say.

Step 3: Pick your learning sprint

Choose one skill, just one, that will expand your options. Maybe it's AI tools, stakeholder engagement or public speaking. Don't overthink it. Follow what feels relevant and interesting.

Block out at least 30 minutes a day, five days a week (or as much time as you can create). It doesn't need to be perfect. You just need to begin and stick with it!

Step 4: Do the work

Now it's about showing up — not perfectly, but consistently. That's when doing the work matters most. Consistency builds something deeper than just results; it builds trust in yourself, and that trust fuels belief, momentum and the determination to keep going when things get uncomfortable. This is your life, your future, and you get to choose how you show up for it.

One thing I know for sure is that if you want to stay relevant and fulfilled in this ever-changing world of work, you need to make learning a lifelong habit. The people who will thrive over the next decade and beyond are the ones willing to keep showing up, ask better questions, learn new tools, and evolve with the world around them.

(continued)

If you're looking for a more tailored roadmap — whether you're aiming for a promotion, thinking about switching industries or exploring the idea of starting your own thing — I've created a tool to support you. Alongside this book, I've built Pivotr, an AI-powered career mentor designed to help you map out your next steps with clarity and confidence. It's practical, personalised and built to meet you exactly where you are, while teaching you the skills to future-proof your career.

Head to pivotr.com to get your pivoting plan today, and be sure to keep your suitcase topped up, keep learning and, no matter where your next step takes you, take it boldly.

Chapter 7

Building your personal brand

I f you've ever felt overlooked, underappreciated or unsure how to stand out in your industry, this chapter is for you. What I'm about to share is often the missing piece in a successful career strategy: your personal brand. In a crowded market, talent alone is no longer enough. You need to be known. You need to be remembered, and you need to be positioned.

This chapter is your blueprint for doing just that. I walk you through how to present yourself as an expert, build credibility and attract the right opportunities, without posting online multiple times a day or changing who you are. Whatever next bold move you plan on making — whether you're stepping up for a promotion, stepping into a new industry or stepping out to build something of your own — how the market perceives you is no longer optional; it's essential.

I've seen far too many talented career professionals rely on outdated advice to guide these moves. In fact, one of the worst pieces of career advice I've ever heard is still being handed out today: 'Just get your head down and do the work'.

For years, I lived by that advice: work hard, keep my head down and let my results speak for themselves. The problem with this advice is that it doesn't get you seen. In today's world of work, it's not enough to do great work; you need to be known for it.

Let's reframe that old and outdated advice into something that gets results: 'Do the work — and make sure people know you did it'.

Understanding what a personal brand really is

Your personal brand is what people say about you when you're not in the room. It's your reputation, your story and the value you bring. It's the way you show up, online and offline. In a noisy world where opportunities are often shared behind closed doors or in private messages, your personal brand is your shortcut to being remembered and recommended. It's how people know what you stand for, what you're great at and where you're headed.

Whether you realise this or not, you already have a personal brand. So the question is are you in control of it? Building your brand means choosing what you want to be known for, and then showing up consistently, visibly and boldly in that space. When it comes to building your brand, the best place to start is exactly where you are, and conduct a brand audit.

Ask yourself:

- How would others describe you professionally?
- What are you currently known for inside and outside of work?

- What do people come to you for?

- What kind of opportunities are you currently being considered for?

Your answers will give you a baseline and help you see the gap between your current perception and your future intention.

Now, I know what you're thinking, as I have gone on a similar journey myself. *Georgie, what if what I'm known for right now isn't what I want to be known for going forward? I'm ready for a change, ready to pivot, but my current brand reflects my past, not my future?* Great question!

Whether you're shifting industries, stepping into leadership or exploring something entirely new, your personal brand is the one thing that always comes with you, and here's what's important to remember: your brand is not what you do. It's not tied to a job title, a company or an industry. Your personal brand is rooted in who you are, why you do what you do, how you show up and, most importantly, how you make people feel in the process.

That's what people remember. That's what builds trust and that's what moves with you, wherever your career takes you next.

You will outgrow jobs, organisations and even industries like I did when I pivoted out of beauty but, as you now know, what you learn and the skills you gain can all transfer across with you.

In a world where AI can automate tasks, generate content and even screen résumés, what sets you apart isn't what you do but who you are. Your personal brand is your human edge. It's your voice, values, lived experience and ability to build trust — and no technology can replicate that.

I'm not saying you need to become an influencer or post on social media all day, but you do need to become recognisable for the value and insights you offer.

Your personal brand is how you stay relevant, human and in demand, no matter how fast the world changes.

Build confidence to post and share your voice

One of the biggest hurdles in personal branding, especially for many women, is gaining the confidence to put yourself out there. This is why I went into depth at the beginning of the book around impostor syndrome and how this can hold us back unless we learn to coexist with it. Putting yourself out there and beginning to post online or positioning yourself as a leader in your place of work can bring up all types of thoughts and feelings.

Don't think I am immune to any of this. I have had so much fear and anxiety about putting my ideas and thoughts into the world. But here's the thing I always remind myself: it's not about me. It's about the people I want to help. When your messages, content and ideas come from a genuine place, people feel this and will begin to relate and connect with who you are, where you're going and what you stand for. You build a great brand simple by building trust.

I did this when I started building my personal brand. Instead of thinking, *How do I talk about myself without sounding like I'm bragging?* I flipped the script. I asked myself, 'What's the takeaway for someone else reading or hearing this?' For example, rather than leading a post with 'Celebrating eight years in business', I shared, 'Here's what I learned running CH Solutions for the past eight years, and what I'd do differently if I were starting over'.

As you can see, I am still celebrating the moment (and showing my capability), but I am also giving value. I'm sharing the lesson, not just the win. That slight mindset shift made it less about me and more about what others can learn, and by sharing my own experiences in a way that offers value to the marketplace, I stopped feeling like an impostor.

Sharing content in this way has enabled me to build a trusted brand, which has led to a number of opportunities that would not have happened if I had not put my voice, value and perspective online. The more I showed up, the more opportunities came my way.

Over the past eight years, I've been invited to speak at industry events, secured new business, attracted top-tier talent and built a powerful network that continues to open doors I never imagined.

So now it's your turn. It's time to stop playing small and begin using your voice to build your reputation and brand both inside and outside your place of work.

Use your voice inside your workplace

When it comes to building a personal brand, let's start with the internal. Don't neglect where you are and the rooms you're already in. This is incredibly important, because visibility leads to opportunity. Throughout my recruitment career, I have witnessed firsthand that it's not always the most capable person who gets the promotion or leads the next project. It's the person who's seen, who's known and who others trust to lead.

Once you know what you want to be known for, it's time to think about how you will get noticed and showcase your unique value in the world.

Here are some ways you can start building internal visibility:

- *Speak up in meetings:* Ask a question, share a perspective and let people hear your thinking.

- *Put your hand up:* Look for projects that align with the brand you want to be known for.

- *Be visible in the right rooms:* Attend team meetings, town halls and cross-functional groups.

- *Offer value:* Mentor someone, present what you've learned or lead a session.

- *Think about your intro:* How you introduce yourself sets the tone for how others see you.

- *Connect with people in your place of work:* Show curiosity in what they do.

Remember, more visibility equals more opportunity. The following figure outlines some of the opportunities that can emerge once you're more visible.

Once you begin building your brand internally, consider these questions to help shape your identity within the four walls of your place of work:

- If someone in your company had to describe you to a leader, what would they say?

- Would they say the things you want to be known for?

- Would you be first in mind for any new opportunities or promotions?

- If a restructuring happened, would your role be secure?

Skilled but **Unseen**	Skilled but **Visible**
Talents go unnoticed	'I thought of you for this role.'
Limited recognition	'I'd love you to speak at our event.'
Waiting for chances	'I have this amazing opportunity for you.'
Career feels stagnant	'You should apply for this promotion'

Moving from unseen to visible and gaining opportunities

If you don't like the answers, it's time to shift that narrative through consistently showing up, speaking up and staying visible. It's also important to ensure you stay relevant and updated with the latest technology advancements.

I outline the hard and human skills required for the next ten years in detail in chapter 5, so be sure to update your skill set and showcase what you are learning and how this could benefit your company now and into the future.

You can be brilliant at what you do, and have all the latest and greatest skills, but if no-one knows it, you won't move your career forward. Visibility isn't ego; it's leverage. Trust me when I say it matters more than ever.

Use your voice outside your workplace

If people only know you within your company, you're missing out on so many opportunities.

Your personal brand shouldn't be constrained to just your place of work; it should also live beyond it, because, as just outlined, opportunities flow to people who are visible.

The panels, the podcast invites, the 'I thought of you for this role' or the message from a recruiter like me outlining an amazing opportunity — those all come when people outside your organisation know who you are and what you do.

So, how do you build that kind of visibility? You can start by showing up on social media platforms such as LinkedIn — again, not to impress, but to share value.

So many platforms are available, but when it comes to building your brand, think about where your audience hangs out the most. If you are a career professional, that's LinkedIn. I have been using LinkedIn since I started my recruitment career over 12 years ago. The platform has changed dramatically over that time. What used to be just a recruitment tool is now so much more. It is your professional online stage, it's your online résumé, and it's where I want you to focus your energy when it comes to building your brand.

Recruiter insight: How we use LinkedIn to discover bold talent

I am going to let you in on all the secrets now, because I want you to be successful and, to do that, you need to be seen and searchable.

When a recruiter, hiring manager or any talent professional receives a résumé, they will visit your LinkedIn profile. This is why you need to set up your online profile for credibility.

When I click on someone's profile, I look for professionalism and that the CV I have received matches the person's online profile. I will look at your picture and want to ensure it's professional. I will read the text underneath your picture, your bio, and look over the jobs you have had throughout your career.

I will also look over any recent posts you have shared to see what you care about, and if you have any testimonials to back up the work you have done. If I like what I see and your skills seem a good match for the role I am recruiting for, I will call you. This is why it's so important to think about your online brand. Like I said at the start of this chapter, we all have a personal brand; it's just how you present yourself in this digital world we live in.

The other way recruiters find talent is by headhunting. I don't wait for CVs to come into my inbox, but instead actively engage with great talent through LinkedIn Recruiter. What I am about to tell you is extremely important if you want to be discovered and have opportunities knocking on your door.

Thanks to new technology advancements, matching talent to positions has never been easier. I can now upload a job description into LinkedIn Recruiter, and AI will source the profiles of people who match that description. This has been a game changer in recruitment and saves the CH Solutions team and me a lot of time and energy. We will then call the top profiles and begin our process.

But here's the important bit: the only way you show up at the top of those results is if your profile matches what the AI is searching for. That means your LinkedIn profile, headline, about section, experience and skills list need to contain the right keywords, language and focus.

(continued)

If your profile doesn't reflect what you want to be found for, you won't be surfaced in any searches, even if you're the perfect fit. This is why your online profile is increasingly important. Whether you're actively looking or just want to stay visible, make sure your profile speaks clearly to the roles, topics and positions you want to be associated with. To help you think about this easily and practically, you can do a few things.

The first thing is to ensure all your skills (especially the ones you want to be known for) are mentioned in your profile. They can be woven in through your bio, or mentioned like you would in your CV in the experience section. This is what AI will be pulling from, so in this new world, you don't just need a good profile; you also need a searchable one.

The second tip is to look at the jobs or industries you want to move towards. Ask yourself:

- What keywords come up again and again?

- What tools, systems or frameworks are they asking for?

- How do they describe the type of person they're looking for?

This doesn't mean filling your profile with buzzwords. It means being intentional. If you want to pivot into project management and every ad you read mentions 'customer journey mapping' or 'cross-functional teams' and 'stakeholder alignment', ask yourself: can you demonstrate those skills with examples from your current role, even if you haven't held that exact title?

If the answer is yes, great — add these skills to your profile in a way that feels authentic and aligned. Your profile needs to reflect where you're going, not just where you've been.

Finally, make sure you include any relevant qualifications you have. Whether you've completed a short course, a formal qualification or just wrapped up a certification in a new area (such as AI, leadership, or diversity, equity and inclusion), make sure it's visible on your LinkedIn profile.

So many people forget this step, and it really matters. You can add these recent qualifications under education, mention them in your about section, include them in your experience if relevant to a specific role, and include them in your title or headline. For example:

Project Manager | AI Certified | Building Tech that Puts People First

This helps LinkedIn's AI instantly connect you to the right people and opportunities.

I want you to remember a key takeaway: if it's not on your profile, it doesn't count. If you've done the work and got the skills, make sure these are reflected throughout your professional profile.

Knowledge is power, so now that you know this, it's time to take action and improve your LinkedIn profile.

Quick LinkedIn profile checklist

Run through the following checklist to ensure your LinkedIn profile is doing all it can to build your personal brand.

Headline:

☐ Is it more than just your job title?

☐ Does it include keywords you want to be found for?

☐ Can it hint at your expertise or mission?

For example:

- People and Culture Lead | DEI Advocate | Future of Work
- Sales Director | AI Certified | Helping Tech Start-ups Scale Smarter
- Senior Software Engineer | Building Ethical AI | Mentor for Women in Tech

About section:

☐ Does it clearly say what you do, how you do it and why it matters?

☐ Is your tone authentic and easy to read?

☐ Have you mentioned your core skills or career direction?

Experience:

☐ Are your achievements written in a way that shows impact (not just duties)?

☐ Have you tied in relevant keywords from roles you want next?

☐ Does each role reflect what you want to be known for?

Skills and endorsements:

☐ Have you updated your top skills to match where you're heading?

☐ Are your human and hard skills listed?

☐ Have you endorsed others (and asked for a few in return)?

Certifications and courses:

☐ Have you added relevant training, microcredentials or industry certs?

☐ Are you highlighting these qualifications in your headline or about section if relevant?

Photo and banner:

☐ Is your photo recent, clear and professional?

☐ Does your banner image reflect your field, brand or values?

Bonus:

☐ Have you posted, commented or engaged this week? (I dive into this next.)

☐ Does your profile reflect where you're going, not just where you've been?

Standing out online with the BOLD posting formula

Once your profile is set up for success, it's time to bring more people to it and build credibility. This is where posting content comes into play. At the start of this chapter, I spoke about how people have the wrong mindset towards building their personal brand. Where I see so many go wrong is making everything about them, and not thinking about the person who is reading the post. This is where the BOLD posting formula will help you build your brand with clarity and confidence.

The BOLD posting formula involves four clear elements:

1. *Be seen and searchable:* Visibility is step one — if you want to be seen, ensure you're easy to find.

2. *Own your narrative:* Don't let others define your brand; show up as the expert you are and what you want to be known for.

3. *Lead with value:* Offer something helpful, honest or thought-provoking.

4. *Do it consistently:* Posting once isn't enough; posting regularly is where trust and brands are built.

Let's break these down.

Be seen and searchable

Opportunities will no longer go to the most experienced person. They will be offered to the person who's visible, comes to mind first and who's easy to find. With LinkedIn now using AI to match people to roles based on profile data, content and keywords, being both seen and searchable has never mattered more.

This is why I can't stress enough how important it is to set your LinkedIn profile up for success. You want people to land on your profile and know who you are, what you do and what you stand for within the first 60 seconds. Be sure to use the LinkedIn profile checklist just provided to ensure your profile is set up properly.

Think of your profile as being your digital shopfront. Setting it up well is like having clear signage; it tells people what you do and why they should care. But a great shopfront means nothing if no-one walks past it. This is where the next few steps in the bold formula come in.

Own your narrative

Whether you've been intentional about it or not, people already have a sense of who you are, what you stand for and what you bring to the table. I said at the start of the chapter that we all have a personal brand. The question is are you shaping that story?

Every post you write, every meeting you speak in and every introduction you give all add up. It tells people how to see you, how to remember you and, ultimately, whether they think of you when the next opportunity comes along.

So, if you want to be known for something, step up into a new role or industry or even begin building a name for yourself, you have to own your narrative. This is where you take control and decide how you show up in the world, both online and offline. Once you do so, your personal brand won't be built by accident; it will be built by the choices you make, the things you do, and the ideas and stories you choose to share.

Make people remember you for what you want to be known for. That is within your power to shape and mould, but it won't happen overnight. You need to build trust — and that's where the next step in the formula comes in.

Lead with value

When it comes to posting online and building a personal brand, building trust and leading with value is one of the most important steps to think about. The goal when showing up online is to connect, contribute and add value to the conversations that matter to you or your industry.

Whenever you post, ask yourself, 'What's in it for them?' or 'How is this helpful?' Leading with this value-based approach will build trust and help you stand out in a crowded online space.

Here are some easy ways to get going:

- Share something you've learned recently, such as a microcredential you gained or a key takeaway from a talk or podcast.

- Reflect on a challenge you've navigated and what it taught you. This is a great way to showcase your resilience and adaptability.

- Celebrate a small win with a lesson. Your start point could be the course you took, the network event you attended or a recent project milestone moment.

- Ask a question you've been thinking about. This is a great way to spark conversation and connection.

- Highlight someone else's work that inspired you. This is a great way to build your online network with respected career professionals.

- Share an article you have read relevant to your industry with your biggest takeaways.

If you are still struggling to come up with ideas, ask ChatGPT to come up with some, but don't copy what it gives you! Use AI as a sounding board and to help you brainstorm some topics to spark your creativity, but don't copy and paste what it spits out.

People can tell when AI has written a post, so be sure to write it in your own words.

Trust me when I say the need for authenticity and realness is going to become increasingly craved, and those who show up as themselves will gain the most credibility and build the most trusted brands.

When it comes to posting value-based content, always lead with the motivation of 'what can I give' instead of 'what can I get'. If you have this approach, the market will respond to you in a really positive way, leading to more opportunities flowing your way.

But this formula will only work long-term if you apply the final step — consistency.

Do it consistently

Posting once in a blue moon is better than not posting at all, but if you really want to be seen, stand out and be top of mind, you need to be consistent.

Showing up on a regular basis builds trust and shows people you are passionate about what you do and have value to give. It also reinforces your narrative and shapes the story for what you want to be known for. You don't need to post every day or try to go viral; you just need to keep showing up with purpose and on brand.

This could look like:

- posting one to three times a week

- commenting on three relevant posts a week

- blocking 30 minutes to batch ideas for the month ahead.

Whatever your version of 'consistent' looks like, stick to it. Repetition builds recognition, consistency builds credibility, and both build the kind of brand people don't forget.

Building your online network

The final step in building your personal brand is putting yourself out there and surrounding yourself with like-minded career professionals. One thing I have come to realise from investing a lot of time and energy into both my brand and network is this: your brand will get you noticed, but your network will open the right doors and opportunities.

In recruitment, the right network is everything. I wouldn't be where I am today if I hadn't consistently invested in building genuine relationships, especially with the decision makers I now get to partner with. These connections weren't accidental. They were built through trust, value and showing up, again and again. This will not stop. I will continue to invest heavily in building relationships for the rest of my career, and I encourage you to do the same.

When some people think of networking, they still imagine walking into a room of strangers and trying to awkwardly strike up a conversation in the hope of swapping business cards. Don't worry — I am not going to tell you to do that!

Rather than treating networking like speed dating at a meet-up, hoping you randomly bump into someone who could change your life, I want you to have a strategic approach and take a longer term view. The key to networking (as with everything else we've discussed so far) is seeking clarity around what you want to achieve.

By now you might be thinking about pivoting into a more tech-focused role. You've started doing the work, including upskilling, identifying your transferable skills, building your brand and getting clear on the direction you want to head in. The next step is to start building the right network around you, so when the right opportunity shows up, you're already top of mind.

Here's how to begin:

1. Search for recruiters who specialise in the space you're moving into. Head to the LinkedIn Jobs section, find roles that interest you and take note of who posted the ad. Then start connecting with headhunters in that space.

2. Connect with people already in the role you want. Look up professionals who hold the job title you're aiming for, especially those in your local area, and start connecting to a few each week.

3. Follow and connect with target companies. Look at the businesses hiring for the skills you're developing. Connect with their internal talent teams, HR managers and even a few senior leaders in departments relevant to your goal. This is a great step and will begin to build your online network with the right types of people.

Once you have begun building your network, begin engaging with any content they post. Ensure you like, share or even leave a thought-provoking comment about what you learned from any industry-relevant news and posts. These small moves add up and, over time, get you noticed by the right people.

The key is to support your network through being a giver not a taker. Celebrate others' milestones, write a recommendation, endorse someone's skill or share job openings. The more you give without expectation, the more people will naturally gravitate back toward you. Women especially benefit from amplifying each other. So, comment on her post, share her article and keep building others up, because that's what gets you noticed in the long run.

Building up your brand and network takes time, but they are both so essential, especially if you want to stand out and have a long successful career.

Taking your networking offline

The final piece of the puzzle is taking your online connections offline, into real life. I genuinely believe this is what people will crave more and more as the world becomes increasingly digital. Personally, I thrive when I'm around people; it lifts me and, in my opinion, this is where the real, deep relationships are formed. Real relationships aren't formed over a LinkedIn DM, through email, or via a phone call or Slack message; they're formed face to face, human to human. That's where the real connection happens.

When it comes to in-person networking events, you don't need to attend a huge number each month. Instead, be intentional and choose one or two a quarter that pique your interest. Look at the topics being discussed, the panel speakers and who is posting about the event. Have a look at who else might be attending. You could even share potential events with the network you are building, asking if anyone is going along.

Once you've locked in the networking events you want to attend, it's time to focus on making a strong first impression. Remember — this is your brand in motion. How you show up, what you say, how you act and how you present yourself all tell a story. Yes, be yourself, because authenticity is key, but also be intentional. Think about how you want to come across, who you want to connect with and what types of companies you want to attract.

I know walking into a room of strangers can be super intimidating, which is why going prepared is key. I like to go with a quick opening intro, followed by a question. For example, 'Hi, I'm Georgie. It's so nice to meet you. I love coming to events like this and hearing what others are working on. What brought you along tonight?' It's simple, but warm and friendly and always opens up a nice conversation.

Once you have introduced yourself to a number of people in the room, always follow up with a connection request on LinkedIn. This is where your online brand is so key. If your profile looks professional, people will want to connect with you even more.

In-person networking is where your personal brand truly comes alive. It's one thing to create a great profile or post online, but when you walk into a room, how you carry yourself, how you connect and the energy you bring is what people remember.

You don't need a polished pitch; instead, show up with clarity on what you stand for and curiosity about the people around you. When you start building real connections face to face, everything shifts. Trust is built and opportunities are shared — and your brand moves from something people see and read online to something they feel. Trust me when I say that's where the doors blow wide open.

Building your bold personal brand

Let's put everything from this chapter—including your brand, your voice, and your visibility—into action. It's time to begin building your brand, one bold move at a time.

Choose a small move to take this week:

- Update your LinkedIn profile using the checklist provided in this chapter.

- Post your first piece of content using the BOLD posting formula.

- Sign up for a local event—something that gets you in the room.

- Comment meaningfully on a post that aligns with your brand.

- Share an article you have read with your thoughts and biggest takeaway.

- Invite someone in your network for a virtual coffee and genuine conversation.

Your personal brand is already being shaped. You can control the narrative or allow the market to do that for you. This is your chance to own, live and let people feel your brand—one bold move at a time.

Chapter 8

Leading
with confidence

I couldn't write a book about making bold moves without addressing the leadership gap. While women are graduating at higher rates, starting businesses and transforming industries from the inside out, we're still not equally represented at the tables where the biggest decisions are made, and that bothers me.

In this chapter, I explore why the leadership gap still exists and, more importantly, how we can close it. You'll get the 'lay of the land', including the current stats, the barriers that too often hold women back and the real reasons many hesitate to step forward. I also explore what it truly means to 'own the room' — not just in title or tone, but in presence, posture and the quiet confidence that speaks even when you don't. I outline how to negotiate your worth with clarity and conviction, sidestepping self-doubt and stepping into your full value. And I unpack the roles of mentors and sponsors, covering who they are, why they matter and how they can contribute to your growth.

If you're eyeing your next promotion, in the following sections I walk through how to position yourself as a leader before anyone formally hands you the title. This is a big chapter, full of practical insight and powerful mindset shifts. So let's dive in.

Owning the room

I have had the privilege of working with some incredible leaders throughout my career. What makes these women stand out is not only what they say or do, but also how they show up. They all have presence. Whether they're stepping onto a stage, walking into a boardroom, or ordering a coffee at their local café, they show up with a certainty that says, 'I belong here'. Rather than being loud or showy, this is the kind of presence that turns heads without needing to demand attention. A woman who truly owns the room is magnetic. And the more women embody these traits, the more others will follow.

I've been reflecting on this a lot lately. Imagine if we all started backing each other a little more — championing each other, sharing what we've learned and pulling each other up along the way. That's how we shift things. That's how we build something better for the next generation.

Let's learn from women who lead with clarity and confidence, and watch how they carry themselves, speak and lead, because that kind of presence is built, practised and earned — and, more importantly, can be learned.

So, how does a woman like this own the room? Here's what I've noticed. Before she even enters the room, she's already leading. She grounds herself with intention, aligning her posture and walking in with calm power, not anxious energy. Her language is clear and decisive — no 'just', no 'sorry', no qualifiers that dilute her authority. She's not afraid of silence; in fact, she uses it. A well-timed pause becomes her power move, often saying more than an avalanche of words ever could. She reads the room with emotional intelligence, adjusting her tone, bringing others into the conversation, dissolving tension and building trust. And, through it all, she is unapologetically herself, not mimicking anyone else's leadership style or softening her edges. She leads as her whole self and, in doing so, gives everyone around her permission to do the same.

I am sure a woman has come to mind as you read that last paragraph, so here's what I also want you to know. These traits aren't reserved for the chosen few; they're things we can all practise, build and grow into. If you've ever looked at a woman in a leadership role and thought, I wish I could show up like that, know that you can, and you need to, now more than ever. We need more women in the C-suite, leading companies, shaping technology and in the room where the decisions get made. This matter is urgent and, as you are about to read, needs immediate attention.

The stats don't lie

Let's take a look at the reality of where we're at, because the numbers make it impossible to ignore. In Australia, only about one in five CEOs is female, according to 2024 data from the Workplace Gender Equality Agency (WGEA). Despite the fact that women make up around 51 per cent of the Australian workforce, we're still massively underrepresented in leadership across almost every industry. As of the latest WGEA data, women hold just 22 per cent of CEO roles nationally, and only 37 per cent of key management positions, a gap that has barely shifted in recent years.

When we look at boardrooms, the picture isn't much better. Women occupy about one-third of board seats in the private sector, and just 18 per cent of board chair roles, according to WGEA. And at the highest levels of corporate Australia, the gender gap widens even further. In ASX300 companies (the top 300 publicly listed companies), only 9 per cent of CEOs are women, according to the Australian government's *Status of Women Report Card 2024*. That's not just a gap. That's a canyon.

Even in middle management, where you would hope more progress was being made, the numbers tell a different story. According to McKinsey & Company's *Women in the Workplace 2023* report, conducted in partnership with LeanIn.Org, just two in every five managers are women. This highlights the issue of leadership pipeline leaks occurring long before women reach executive roles.

This is one of the reasons I am so passionate about sponsorship and mentorship. As the co-founder of the Big Sister Mentorship program, I have seen firsthand the progress that can be made when women help other women. The more we support one another, the faster we can close the gap. We also need our male allies. I don't know about you, but some of the biggest supporters across my career have been male, so it's important to remember we can't do it alone.

One thing is for sure: the leadership gap isn't about a lack of talent, drive or ambition. It's about systems that weren't built with women in mind, and cultures that still don't always make space for women to lead.

So, what are the barriers for women? I have been diving deep into this topic, because I am curious by nature and wanted to get to the root of this core issue. Now that you are ready to make your bold move, you need to be aware of the invisible barriers surrounding you so you can navigate them with confidence.

Barriers to women's leadership

The lack of women in leadership isn't about lack of capability or ambition; it's about the systems we're navigating that weren't built with us in mind. Women face a combination of structural barriers, cultural biases and internal obstacles that slow us down or shut us out completely.

I caught up with a great friend the other day, and we discussed this very topic. I'll call her Emily. Emily works for a global brand and is part of the senior leadership team. She is one of the most driven, hard-working, intelligent women I know, and recently got a promotion. Life always tests us, however, and when Emily rang me she felt like the weight of the world was on her shoulders — and no wonder. A family member had just been diagnosed with a serious illness, and Emily was doing all she could to support them. To make matters more complex, this family member currently looked after Emily's four-year-old daughter two days a week but, due to her diagnosis, could no longer do this for the foreseeable future. Emily had tried to get an extra two days in day care for her daughter, but could only get one extra day.

Emily had no choice but to reduce her work week from five days to four. When she explained this to her employer, she could sense they were displeased, and she began feeling judged.

A couple of her male counterparts (who were definitely not male allies) made some snide comments during the days she was in the office, and she began to feel isolated from the team she had built around her.

I wish I could say Emily's story is unique, but it's not. It's a prime example of how workplaces were designed around a version of leadership that assumed no career breaks, no caregiving responsibilities, and a full-time worker who could stay late, show up early and always be 'on'. That model doesn't reflect the reality of most women's lives.

This version of leadership means that when women step back even slightly from full-time work, they're often overlooked for high-visibility projects, leadership pathways or promotions. They don't lack the required skills, but they just don't get the opportunities.

On top of all this, the incorrect assumption still exists that just because a woman has children, she's less committed to her career. I've seen the opposite. I've watched my female friends step into bigger roles, earn more money and push harder because they want to provide a fantastic life for their children and be outstanding role models. They don't lack ambition. They just need flexible work policies that allow them to lead both at home and in the workplace.

Then there's the 'judged if you do, invisible if you don't' dilemma, which is probably the most exhausting and hardest to navigate. It goes like this: be warm and likeable, but don't be too nice, because people will walk all over you. I quickly learned the hard way from doing this, so I went in the opposite direction and became assertive and direct. Nope, that didn't work either. I was coming across as too aggressive and arrogant. At one point in my life, I honestly felt that I couldn't win. The irony is that the qualities praised in male leadership — including directness, drive and decisiveness — are often frowned upon in women.

Oh, and let's not forget the 'old boys' club'. It's not just a metaphor; it's been a very real dynamic for decades. I've experienced it firsthand, and especially while working in a male-dominated industry for over ten years.

I remember one particular client Pam and I had where we were one of two agencies on their recruitment panel. We knew exactly which other agency they were using, and we noticed a pattern: their job ads would always go live 24 hours before we even received the roles. One day, we decided to call it out and asked why we were consistently behind. It turns out that the director of the company we were recruiting for and the director of the other agency would catch up mid-week over a pint. And, of course, in the director's exact words, 'Work comes up!'.

This was a classic example of how male networks operate. Business often happens outside the boardroom, and having access to these conversations is a significant advantage. These informal connections still shape opportunities today.

Finally, let's talk about the internal barriers that hold us back, which I hope by now you are beginning to work through. It's heartbreaking to think about the number of women I've spoken to who've said, 'I don't feel ready' or 'I don't think I'm qualified enough', even when they're more than ready. That's impostor syndrome in action.

I was recently recruiting for a technical lead role for one of my recruitment clients. Whenever I am headhunting for a leadership position, I always make a conscious effort to deliver a diverse shortlist. I made two calls to potential candidates, one after another. The first was with an experienced female leader who had worked in tech for over a decade. She was more than qualified for the role; however, the more depth I went into about the opportunity, the more she started talking herself out of it. She told me, 'I just don't feel ready, Georgie'. Next up, I called a male developer with three years less experience. Not only was he making $10 000 a year more than she was, but he was also so confident that he could do the role, his final words on the call were, 'Georgie, just get me the interview and I can do the rest'. What a contrast!

In my 12 years of recruitment, I have seen women undersell their skills, hesitate before applying for stretch roles and second-guess whether they're 'too much' for asking for what they're worth. Meanwhile, many of their male counterparts throw their hats in the ring before they read the full job description.

As if all of these barriers weren't enough, add in the lack of visible female role models and it's no wonder many women question whether leadership is meant for them. No wonder so many don't even want to put themselves forward in the first place.

However frustrating it can feel, I always remind myself that none of this is fixed. And women like you and me have the power to shift it. The more we talk about these issues, and the more we call them out, the less power they hold. The more we step into leadership, the more we open the door for the next woman to walk through beside us. With every bold move, we chip away at the systems that were never built with us in mind.

Stepping up and leading with confidence

You don't have to wait for things to change to start making bold moves. You can take action right now to step into your power, show up with presence and move forward on your own terms.

The best place to start is through being aware of how you speak. I've worked on this a lot and still do. Hosting a weekly podcast has been one of the best tools for that. When I started listening back to episodes, I experienced so many cringe-worthy moments, full of filler words such as 'umm', 'so', and 'like'. It wasn't easy to hear, but I knew if I wanted to work on my communication, I had to push past the discomfort and notice what needed improving.

Instead of being overly critical, I approached it with curiosity. I started to notice the little habits, such as how often I added qualifiers: 'I just wanted to say' or, 'I'm not sure, but … '. These tiny phrases made my voice and ideas sound smaller, as if I was trying to soften what I was saying before I even said it. The positive from doing this review was that I became aware of it and could change it, and so can you.

Now I know not everyone will have a podcast to listen back to, so if you're wondering where to begin, start by recording a voice note speaking on a topic you want to bring up at work. I do this often before an important meeting. I will practise what I want to say, while recording myself saying it. I will then listen back to it and reflect on the tone, the pace and the words I use.

You can also practise by using the voice function on ChatGPT. Prompt it by saying you want it to act like a top communication and leadership coach and give feedback on your language. I have used this function a lot recently, and it has really helped.

Human feedback is also another great way to improve. Ask a trusted friend or colleague to reflect on what they notice when you speak — not to pick you apart but to give you clarity. Start by asking:

- 'Do I use a lot of filler words, such as "um", "like", "so"?'

- 'Am I qualifying my ideas with "just," "maybe" or "I think"?'

- 'How's my pace? Am I rushing or rambling?'

- 'Does my tone sound confident and clear, or hesitant and unsure?'

The goal isn't perfection; it's to become more intentional so your message lands the way you want it to. Because how you say something matters just as much as what you say.

Once you notice how you speak, the next step is to be aware of your body language. Consider:

- How do you walk into a room?

- How do you sit in a meeting in person or online?

- Do you make eye contact?

- Do you have any bad habits, such as picking your nails or playing with your hair?

Again, your aim is to be aware of how you hold and present yourself. One thing I noticed about myself was that I looked down a lot when I was entering a room or meeting someone for the first time.

Now I make sure I hold my head high, pull my shoulders back and make eye contact with people I want to speak with. This progress has come from consistently working at it and being prepared.

When I've felt the least confident, it's never been because I wasn't capable; I just wasn't prepared. When it comes to owning the room, preparation is everything if you want to nail that meeting, presentation or pitch. Know your stuff, practise delivering it and get comfortable with your message, so it feels like second nature.

And when nerves show up (because they will), ground yourself in the facts. Remind yourself of the wins you've already had. Stack the evidence that you are great at what you do, and remember that you're not just meant to be in the room, you're also meant to own it.

If you're not sure how you're coming across, again, ask someone you trust to give you feedback. This has been really powerful for me, and I am grateful to have some wonderful friends and a husband who can be both my fans and advisers. If you don't have that person or people in your life right now, look for meet-ups or join a program such as Toastmasters, like I did. I promise you won't regret it.

Preparing for promotion and making your bold move

Once you're more aware of how you present yourself, it's time to prepare your bold move. Doing great work is essential, especially if you want to step up into a bigger role and lead. However, visibility is as important as performance. I have seen and heard far too many women stay stuck in the middle because they assume that their hard work will speak for itself. Sitting there waiting for someone to spot your potential is not a winning strategy, and will rarely lead to the outcome you want. You don't need to brag, but you do need to make sure your accomplishments are visible and take credit for your work.

Let's explore how to do this.

Deliver results

Firstly, start where you are, and deliver excellence in your current role. This is such an important first step. Your aim should be to become the person people can rely on to get the job done. As you do this, keep track of all your wins, feedback and results. Write them all down at the end of each week. This is important not just for your confidence, but also for when that promotion opportunity comes up. If you have regular one-on-ones or check-ins with your manager, use them to share your progress. Keep them in the loop on what you're working on and where you're adding value.

For example:

- 'I've been consistently hitting or exceeding my monthly targets, and last quarter I brought in two new key clients.'

- 'The initiative I led hit 110 per cent of its goal.'

- 'The team delivered the project ahead of schedule and under budget.'

Again, this is about showcasing your results, rather than bragging.

Ask for what you want

Don't assume your manager knows that you want to step up; you need to let them know. In your next catch-up, you could simply say, 'I'm interested in moving into a leadership role. What do I need to focus on to get there?' This will open up a good conversation while making them aware of where you want to go and what you want to achieve. Don't wait until you feel ready; own your ambition and showcase this to your manager, so they start to think of you when opportunities come up.

Take stretch opportunities

As I have continued to repeat throughout this book, growth and confidence never come from staying in your comfort zone. They come from having the courage to put your hand up and say yes to a new opportunity that will stretch you slightly. If a project needs structure, a process needs fixing or a team needs direction, offer to take it on. If no-one steps forward, be the one who does. You'll not only build new skills, but also give others a chance to see you in action, and usually outside your immediate team. That's how sponsors are created.

Find your advocates, mentors and sponsors

Mentors are essential; they help guide, advise and support you. I would not be where I am today without my mentors. Importantly, they have helped guide me the most when I am second-guessing myself or just need some clarity on what my next move could look like. I can't speak highly enough of mentors, and if you can mentor someone, do it, because you learn so much as a mentor and a mentee.

A mentor can be from both inside and outside of your organisation, and the latter is powerful because you can gain a different perspective from outside of the four walls of your company. A mentor doesn't even need to be someone you know personally. I look to people who inspire me and are achieving things I also want to achieve. If they have a book, I will read it. If they have a podcast, I will listen to it. If they run events, I will do my best to attend them. I will absorb as much from them as I can. Mentors also don't have to be far-off executives or industry icons. They can simply be someone a few steps ahead of where you want to go.

Once you've identified particular mentors, reach out to them. Try a personalised message on LinkedIn in which you share what you admire about their work and ask if they'd be open to sharing how they got started. Keep it genuine and respectful. If they work in the same company, send them a quick email letting them know you're keen to learn, and offer to grab a coffee. Most people are more than happy to share their story — you just have to ask.

Another form of advocates are sponsors, and these are different from mentors. They're the people who say your name in rooms you're not in. They're the ones who help make promotions happen.

In *Forget a Mentor, Find a Sponsor*, economist Sylvia Ann Hewlett argues women with sponsors are 20 per cent more likely to be promoted or get a raise. This means that one relationship could change everything. So how do you get a sponsor? Well, you don't simply walk up to them and say, 'Hey, can you sponsor me?' It's something that grows through trust and visibility.

Start by focusing on the first three areas just discussed — deliver excellence, ask for what you want and take on new projects that get you noticed. Put your hand up for high-impact programs. Lead where you can, get results and make sure the right people are seeing them.

Then, build relationships. Don't just stick to your own lane or team; find ways to connect with senior leaders. If someone gives you good feedback, follow up. Keep them in the loop and show them what you're working on.

Finally, be clear about where you want to go. Say things like, 'I'm really focused on growing into a leadership role. I'd love your perspective on how I'm tracking'. That puts you on their radar without asking for anything formal.

At the end of the day, sponsorship is about people backing those they believe in, based on the evidence they've been given.

Fill the gaps, before they're gaps

Look up or across to where it is you want to go. Ask yourself:

- What do those leaders know?

- What are they responsible for?

- How do they present themselves?

Whether it's managing budgets, leading teams or communicating vision, start developing those skills now. Take a short course, ask to shadow someone or offer to lead a meeting. Show initiative and act before you feel ready, so when the time comes, impostor syndrome can quickly be shut down, because you won't be faking it till you make it. You will have done the work and be ready to step up or into that new position.

Know your worth, and ask for it

Once you have taken the five key steps outlined in the preceding sections and begun to step up, it's time to talk about money. When you continue to work on yourself—upskilling, re-skilling and knowing your stuff—you also deserve your pay to reflect your work.

Unfortunately, too many women don't get paid their worth. According to WGEA, as of 2024, the average total remuneration gender pay gap in Australia is 21.8 per cent. That means, for every dollar a man earns, a woman earns just 78 cents. Over a year, that adds up to a staggering $28 425 less for women doing comparable work.

Knowing your worth is one part of the equation; asking for it is the other.

Negotiation is a powerful skill you can work on and, for many women, one of the most underused. The first step is a mindset shift. Remove emotion and focus on the facts and the value you bring. Before you start the conversation, know your numbers and do your research. Know what your role is worth in the market. Next, make a note of all your results. Have you led a team or a large program of work? Have you increased revenue, launched a new product line, saved time or delivered anything of impact? Write down everything you've achieved.

You're not asking for a pay rise because you 'deserve' more. You're asking because you've earned it. Again, this goes back to preparation and practise. Once you have everything written down and you know what you want to say, it's time to role-play how you say it. Rehearse your ask until it feels natural. Keep your tone confident and collaborative, not apologetic. Say something like:

Based on my performance this past year and the market range for this role, I'd like to discuss adjusting my compensation to reflect the value I'm bringing.

Your discussion doesn't need to be overly scripted; stick to the facts and the results you have delivered for the business. Once you have made your ask, don't rush to fill the silence; stop and let them respond. That pause might feel uncomfortable, but it often leads to your best leverage. Silence is a powerful tool, so use it.

If you get pushback, remain calm, don't get emotional and stay factual. You can respond with something like, 'What would it take for me to get to that number or achieve this goal?' This keeps the door open, invites collaboration and shows you're serious.

Negotiation isn't just about salary, either. You could discuss equity, bonuses, extra leave, flexibility, leadership training or a clearer path to promotion.

The more you practise such discussions, the more natural they become. Keep making those notes on all your progress and wins. Doing so will not only improve your chance of promotion when the time comes, but also continue to boost your self-belief.

This isn't just about you, either. Every time you advocate for yourself, you give another woman permission to do the same. And every time you don't, you keep the gap in place. So let's not play small here — we've worked too hard to settle for anything less than what we are worth.

Leading with confidence in the future of work

The path to leadership isn't always easy, but it is necessary. When women lead, workplaces thrive, cultures shift and the systems that once held us back begin to change.

If you're already in a leadership role, never doubt your ability — you've earned your seat. Don't ever forget that your voice, lens and leadership style are needed, especially now as we enter a new era of work. In a world in which change is the only constant, we don't need more of the same. We need leaders who bring emotional intelligence, inclusive thinking and human-centred leadership to the table, and that's exactly where women thrive. As you rise, don't forget to sponsor another woman. Open doors, and say her name in rooms she's not in yet. Even the smallest moments of support can change someone's entire path.

For those preparing to lead, an important and needed place exists for you in the future of work. But you can't wait to be chosen; you have to choose yourself first. The tools discussed through this chapter about owning the room, building presence, negotiating your worth and preparing for promotion aren't just nice to have anymore. They're essentials in a world where skills evolve fast, and confidence is the most valuable currency.

AI might be transforming tasks and roles, but it can't replace your vision, your voice and your lived experience. What makes you human — your empathy, creativity and ability to connect and lead with heart — is the edge in this next decade of work. So be bold. Speak up. Advocate for yourself and for others. One woman leading with courage clears the path for many more.

Finding your mentors and sponsors and taking a bold step up the leadership ladder

Let's get practical and apply what you've learned in this chapter to find your next mentor or sponsor.

Step 1: Identify your leadership gap

Think about the kind of leader you want to become in the next 12 to 24 months. What specific skills, opportunities or mindset shifts do you need to get there?

In your journal, device or notepad, write down two to three leadership qualities or experiences you'd like to build — for example, leading a cross-functional team, increasing executive presence, or improving verbal and non-verbal communication skills.

Step 2: Build your mentorship map

Next, draw two columns on a page with the following headings:

- Mentor (guides you)

- Sponsor (advocates for you).

List two to three people in each column. To work out some good options, ask yourself:

- Who inspires you?

- Who is where you want to be?

(continued)

- Who could you build a deeper connection with?

- Who do you want to notice your skills?

Step 3: Take the first bold step

Pick one person on your list and send them a message this week. Keep it simple and respectful — for example:

Hi *[Name]*, I've long admired how you lead with *[specific trait]*. I'm aiming to step into more leadership responsibilities in my own career and would really value a 20-minute chat to learn from your experience. Would you be open to connecting sometime soon?

Take that first bold step towards climbing the leadership ladder.

Chapter 9

Designing a career on your terms

We've journeyed through a lot together in this book — from stories to strategies, and from frameworks to future skills. At the very beginning, I made it clear that this wasn't going to be just another career guide filled with clichés. I set out to create a practical guide for future-proofing your career, one grounded in authenticity, clarity and courage. Because when you are anchored in who you are, clear on what you stand for and confident in your strengths, navigating the next chapter in your career becomes less about guesswork and more about alignment. From that place, momentum can be built — one bold move at a time. Now it's time to craft a vision for your future that doesn't just look impressive from the outside but feels deeply aligned with who you are on the inside.

By the end of this chapter, you will understand what success looks like to you in this season of your life, and how to get on course — and stay on course — no matter where you are currently.

Success and seasons

If you don't define what success means for you, society will do it for you, leading to an unfulfilling career and life. The best thing I ever did was clarify what kind of life and career I wanted, and what felt right to me at that time. I had to be honest about where I was and what was important to me. I often think of life as being divided into seasons, with each one shaped by our circumstances, energy and evolving priorities. Just like nature, we shift, and that's normal. Life and careers are not linear, and they're not meant to be.

When you understand the season you're in, you give yourself permission to redefine what success looks like, on your terms. For example, if you're a new parent, your version of success will look very different today from what it did in your career's early days. If you're launching a business, your energy, focus and goals will shift again. Each season invites a new definition of success, a different version of you and the courage to honour it.

As of now, I know I am in a season of growth, where work is taking priority. I don't want to be out on the weekend trying out the latest bar, or going on long trips away. I find myself saying 'no' a lot — for example, to social events and coffee catch-ups through the week. This isn't because I don't value my friends or am anti-social, but because I know I am in a season of focus.

However, in a previous season of my life, I wanted to travel and be social. I honoured that and, more importantly, enjoyed it. If I had tried to sit down in that season and, say, write this book, I would have found it incredibly challenging, because I wasn't in that energy or phase of life. Now, I can't think of anything more enjoyable than sitting here on a chilly Sunday afternoon, fire on in the background, and writing these very words.

Knowing what season you are in is incredibly powerful. Instead of comparing yourself to someone else's version of success, you ground yourself in yours.

Seasons can be short or long, depending on your focus, and with each bringing its own pace, pressures and purpose. You can also find yourself back in different seasons many times, each one with a more evolved version of yourself, but still in a similar phase of life. The key is recognising where you are now, so you can make decisions that support, rather than sabotage, your current reality.

So what season are you in now? The following sections provide some examples of what seasons of life can look like.

Starting your career and figuring things out

At the start of your career, you're in a season of growth and learning. This is the season when you will want to gain as much knowledge and experience as possible, learn from your seniors and soak up as much as you can. You'll be saying 'yes' to opportunities, being a sponge for new information, and adding as many tools and skills as possible. In this season, you will want to try new things, take some risks and not be afraid to experiment.

Blending career growth with raising young kids

With young kids, flexibility isn't just nice to have; it's essential. Being present at home matters deeply, and having a more predictable routine can be the anchor that keeps everything steady. In this season, you might prioritise security, lean into your strengths, and choose work that feels purposeful and manageable.

That doesn't mean your ambition has disappeared. It's still there, alive and well. But in this season, you're expressing it differently. You're not playing small, you're playing smart. You may choose not to lead the biggest program or go after the next title — not because you can't, but because you're clear on what truly matters right now.

Ambition doesn't always have to be making the boldest move. Sometimes, it involves creating a sustainable rhythm, working smart and preserving energy.

Launching a business or chasing a bold new idea

During this season, you are ready to go full steam ahead and take a few risks. Whether it's launching a new business or acting on a big, bold idea, you're ready to double down on growth and learning. You say yes to opportunities that will move you forward and have the most impact, and no to things that suck your time and energy.

This season is also when you push yourself outside your comfort zone the most, and know that you are in the unknown. It's when you back yourself and do the required work to get you to where you want to be. It's also where you need to balance speed with recovery — otherwise, you risk not making it out of this season in a place of good health.

Rebuilding after a big change

Recovering from disruptive change, such as a move, break-up or job loss, can be a challenging season. Especially as the world speeds up and change is the only constant, this is a season we will all find ourselves in. Do not judge yourself, and instead show compassion and grace.

Blaming others and playing the victim can be easy during this season, so try not to stay in it too long. Courage is key and taking action, however small, each day matters more than trying to overhaul your entire life all at once. Make yourself your number one priority and build trust and belief in yourself again. Slowly step back into your power, before getting behind the driver's seat of your life again and grabbing the wheel with both hands. This season can be the most challenging but is a life-changing one, forcing you to audit your entire life. If you are in this season, remember — it's a chapter, not your story, so don't let anyone else write it.

Exploring and embracing adventure

In this season, you will be craving something new. Maybe you've been working in the same job for the past seven years, or the business you started no longer aligns with where you want to go next. Maybe it's time for a new environment, a move overseas or a new city. You may feel like things have become stagnant, and you have lost the spark you once had. Things that used to challenge you now just bore you. In this season, you need to acknowledge what no longer serves you and take action before you feel ready. Otherwise, you risk being in this season far too long and wondering why life feels out of alignment and unfulfilling.

Preparing to downshift, slow down or give back

In this season, you may be looking to pull back from work, retire and begin leaving your legacy. Finding a sense of purpose during this season of transition is critical. Work plays a significant role in our lives and often shapes our identity. This can be a journey if your self-worth is tied up in 'what' you do, not 'who' you are. Go easy on yourself during this season. Find ways to give back, because this will give you purpose and fulfilment. This could be a season in which you offer to coach or mentor someone, pursue that creative project, get more involved in your community or even take some longer trips. It can be a great season and one where you can really lean in and enjoy.

Of course, more seasons are possible in your life than the ones just outlined, but this gives you an idea of how different seasons can look. Now ask yourself: what season are you in right now?

Write down your thoughts, and seek clarity around where you are, why, and what's important to you in this season. This is such an important step and will make defining your version of success so much easier, because success isn't static. Your definition of success will evolve throughout your life, depending on what stage or season you are in.

The following table summarises the main seasons discussed here, what will likely be your focus and key actions during each one.

How different seasons affect your focus and actions

Season	Focus	Key actions
Starting your career	Learning	Say yes, be a sponge, experiment
Balancing your career and your family	Flexibility and presence	Play smart, find a sustainable rhythm
Launching bold new ideas	Risk and growth	Go full steam, push your comfort zone
Rebuilding after change	Recovery and courage	Show yourself compassion, take small actions daily

Season	Focus	Key actions
Exploring what's next	Adventure and renewal	Acknowledge what no longer serves you
Preparing to downshift	Legacy and purpose	Give back, find new meaning

Redefining success

Now you know what season of life you are in, it's time to shape what success looks like to you, rather than accepting someone else's version.

Defining my version of success was one of the most empowering exercises I've ever done. It kept me grounded, helped me stay focused on what truly mattered, and stopped me from chasing paths that weren't mine to follow. Most importantly, it freed me from comparing myself to people with entirely different values and living through a completely different season of life. As I mention earlier in the book, I used to be quick to compare myself to others who looked like they were achieving more than I was, and this was especially the case when I started CH Solutions. I would look at other agencies with bigger teams, nicer offices and a fancier website and feel like I was falling behind or wasn't good enough.

Thankfully, I caught myself in this comparison wheel before it got out of hand, and I anchored myself in my values and honouring the season I was in. I was in a season of growth and learning. Never having run a business before, I was facing a steep learning curve, one that I knew I had to give time and energy to. I also reminded myself that I had started CH Solutions to align more with my core values of growth and freedom. I wasn't trying to build the biggest recruitment agency in Australia; I was trying to build a mission-driven company that I could feel proud of.

If I hadn't caught myself comparing my journey to someone else's version of success, I could have easily veered down a path that looked good on the outside, but felt completely out of alignment with my goals and values — and paths built on misalignment rarely lead to the right destination.

You could be going full steam ahead; however, if you're going in the wrong direction, you'll end up somewhere that feels completely separate to who you are and what matters most. I don't want this for you, which is why the next section is going to require you to rewrite what your success story looks like, right now in this season of life you are in.

Rewrite your success story from the inside out

You've grown a lot since the start of our journey together and, by now, you may be looking at your career in a whole new light. You may be ready to make your bold career pivot, learn a new skill, step up into a leadership position or even step into a whole new industry. So it only makes sense that your definition of success evolves, as does the story you tell yourself about it.

The following exercise asks you to write your new version of success. Before you do so, however, you must let go of the old story that no longer serves you.

Letting go of the 'old' way to discover the 'bold' way

Take a moment to write and, at the same time, release the old story you'd been telling yourself about success. Ask yourself:

- What did success used to mean to you?

- Where did that definition come from (family, culture, old expectations)?

- How has chasing that version of success affected your career, mindset or wellbeing?

- What part of that story no longer fits?

This is such a powerful place to start, because it brings to life old patterns and beliefs that no longer serve this next chapter and who you are becoming.

Now it's time to anchor yourself in the present and redefine your current version of success. Ask yourself:

- What do you value most in this season of life?

- What does success look like now, on your terms?

- How do you want to feel in your work and life moving forward?

- What are you no longer willing to sacrifice in the name of 'success'?

Let's bring it all together. This is your moment to rewrite your success story, not based on someone else's expectations, but from a place of alignment and intention.

(continued)

Now ask yourself:

- Who are you becoming?

- What kind of person, leader or contributor are you stepping into now?

- What bold move are you ready to make? (This move doesn't have to be huge, but it should feel brave and true.)

- How will you define success moving forward?

Write out your definition of success in one sentence or a short paragraph. Make it yours. Let it reflect this season of your life.

Now ask yourself: what's the first aligned step you will take? Think bold and, most importantly, take action. This is how your next chapter begins — with clarity, courage and one bold move at a time.

Owning your power in a new world of work

This part of the journey has been about more than preparing for the future; it's also been about claiming your place in it.

We began by exploring the skills that will shape the next chapter of work, a mix of hard and human capabilities. In a world where AI and automation are rapidly reshaping industries, technical fluency matters. But just as vital are the deeply human strengths of empathy, adaptability, critical thinking, communication and creativity. These are the traits that will set you apart, no matter the field.

Another important skill is being able to embrace the BOLD pivoting formula from chapter 6. More than simply a roadmap, this is also a mindset. Remember — you don't need the perfect conditions to pivot. You need to start with what you have, where you are, and then take intentional steps forward.

Also keep in mind your transferable skills — those capabilities you've built through real life, not just job titles. They are portable, powerful and often underestimated; owning them is in itself a bold move.

As we navigate this new era of visibility, your personal brand becomes your career currency. It's how you're seen, how you're known and how you attract opportunity. Visibility is not self-promotion but self-leadership. When you stand in your story, you give others permission to do the same. Visibility is a skill and it can be learned. The BOLD posting formula from chapter 7 makes it actionable. This isn't about chasing likes; it's about building trust, showing the world who you are, what you stand for and how you serve. Whether online or in the workplace, the more intentional you are about showing up, the more magnetic your presence becomes.

Women in leadership still face challenges, and it takes courage to rise. You deserve a seat at the table—not later but now, because your voice is needed. Leadership is now about showing up fully and bringing others with you.

And, finally, remember that your definition of success is deeply personal. Success is not a static goal; it's a living, evolving reflection of your values, your season and your vision. Each chapter of your life will call for a different kind of success. Honour that and trust it, and your life and career will continue to flourish.

You now have the tools, the clarity, and the momentum. You've continued to build on your strengthening and now solid foundations. Next up, we look at some examples from career professionals who showcase what bold moves look like in action. I also outline The 30-Day Bold Move Challenge, which brings everything we have journeyed through in this book to life, providing a game plan for 30 days of courageous bold moves and ensuring you are ready for your next challenge.

Let's go!

PART III
YOUR CONFIDENCE BLUEPRINT

Chapter 10

Lessons from the boldest career moves

I'm a big believer that we can't be what we can't see. I started the Sisterhood Club to create spaces where women could come together through events, mentorship and honest conversations on the Career Confidence podcast. I wanted to spotlight the many ways success can look when we back ourselves, take bold moves and say yes before we feel 100 per cent ready.

Over the years, I've had the absolute privilege of sitting down with incredible women and hearing their career journeys firsthand. These stories have stayed with me, not because they were perfect, but because they were real, brave and bold.

Choosing just a handful to include here wasn't easy. But the three stories you're about to read illustrate the very themes we've explored throughout this book: resilience, clarity, alignment, risk and personal power. These stories are proof of what's possible when you trust yourself, know your values and take action from a place of courage.

I've written this book to blend strategy and story because that's how many of us learn best (myself included). So in this chapter, you'll hear from women who made bold career moves and came out the other side stronger, clearer and more aligned with who they are.

Let's look at what bold moves in action looks like.

From hospital shifts to cloud stacks: How Catie boldly rebuilt her career from the ground up

For nearly a decade, Catie Strigenz built a career as a nurse, a role that demanded grit, compassion and the ability to stay composed in unpredictable, high-stakes environments. She worked in neurology units, rose into management, and thrived in the pace of acute healthcare. It was meaningful work. But, over time, the cost started to outweigh the reward.

Physically, the job was taking its toll. Lifting patients, being on her feet for hours and absorbing the stress of other people's emergencies had left her injured and exhausted. And then came the pandemic. During Australia's intense lockdowns, with hospital staff stretched thin, Catie worked relentlessly. Somewhere amid the chaos, a question emerged: 'How long can I do this?' And she meant not just physically but also emotionally, professionally and sustainably.

She wasn't looking to leave nursing straightaway; at this point, the question was only about curiosity.

She didn't let that curiosity leave her, and signed up for a two-week introductory coding course covering HTML and CSS. She went on to build a simple scuba diving webpage, and that's when something clicked. The logic, the structure, the creativity — it all made sense. For the first time, she could picture herself doing something completely different, and not just doing it but being good at it.

That initial course led to another, and then another. She built a quiet momentum behind the scenes, taking boot camps in her downtime while still working shifts at the hospital. But just learning to code wasn't enough; she knew that breaking into tech would require more than technical know-how.

That's where her real edge emerged: the mindset and transferable skills she brought from nursing. These skills included clear communication under pressure, rapid decision making, the ability to stay calm in crisis, and perhaps most importantly, a disciplined, self-directed approach to learning.

Still, the gap between 'can code' and 'employed in tech' was wide. She sent out applications and got silence or rejections. It stung, but she didn't take it personally. 'I treated it like a second job', she said. She tracked her applications, followed up and kept learning. She paced herself and made sure she had some downtime so she could keep showing up, and doing her day job as a nurse to the best of her ability.

After a number of months, she decided to put herself out there and attend a networking event — and this was the turning point. She attended just one meet-up per week and began meeting people in the tech community. This strategy worked as she began to get her brand out there, and people respected what she was doing. At one of those events, she met someone who'd made a similar leap — a

(continued)

former musician turned developer who now spoke at Google events. That moment flipped a switch. 'If she can do it, why can't I?'

At another meet-up, she heard about a traineeship for career switchers and women entering tech, so she applied. 'I just needed to get in the room', she said. 'Once I could talk to people, I knew I could tell my story.' Her story got her the opportunity.

The transition wasn't seamless. She left a leadership role for an entry-level position and had to reorient herself to a new workplace culture. She asked a lot of questions, googled acronyms during meetings and kept her learning curve steep, but she stayed the course.

Today, Catie works as a cloud engineer specialising in Google cloud infrastructure. She also keeps her hand in nursing and still enjoys the impact and purpose this gives her in a more sustainable way.

Her career in health care didn't go to waste. It prepared her for this. She still solves problems and still works in the service of others, just in a different language, one written in code.

Lessons learned: Why Catie's story matters

Catie's story is an example of everything this book stands for.

She didn't have it all figured out. She just knew something needed to change, and she gave herself permission to be curious and explore. Instead of waiting for the perfect plan, she just made one decision — to start before she felt 100 per cent ready.

She backed herself with action. She leveraged her skills — including communication, problem-solving and the ability to stay calm under pressure — and layered in the ones she needed. She showed up to learn, network and keep going, even when the rejections came thick and fast, proving why resilience is key.

This is what a bold move really looks like. It's a quiet, consistent choice to build something better aligned. Catie didn't switch careers to escape; instead, she moved towards a life that fit who she was becoming, what she valued and where her transferable skills were needed.

That's what this work is about: playing to your strengths and making moves, not when it's easy, but when it matters.

From editing pages to leading AI strategy: Lou's bold ascent into a role she wasn't 'qualified' for

Lou Compagnone didn't come from tech. She didn't have a computer science degree or a background in engineering. She came from creative writing, cultural studies and magazine editing. Early in her career, she was writing about food and travel, shaping stories and crafting experiences. But that creative, human-first mindset would provide the exact skill set that positioned her to lead one of the most critical, fast-evolving functions in business today: artificial intelligence.

Lou's shift into tech didn't happen in one dramatic leap; it was layered. As she transitioned from editing to managing digital content, she became more exposed to technology. Curious and adaptable, she followed the thread from content to websites to user experience to service design.

(continued)

Each move pulled her closer to the intersection of humans and systems.

Lou never chased a tech title. She asked better questions. She didn't ask how we could build this faster. She asked, 'Why are we building it at all?' That perspective became her edge, made her visible and got her noticed.

Years before AI hit the mainstream, Lou was already working with business leaders to unpack what was coming, running future-focused strategy sessions, exploring signals of disruption and helping organisations prepare for what was ahead. She wasn't there to sell the hype. She was there to help them think more clearly and more critically. And that's when the opportunity emerged.

As AI rose up the agenda, Lou was already helping teams think through their AI use cases, design for adoption, mitigate risks and centre the human experience. When it came time to define a leadership role for AI, she didn't submit a CV; she was the obvious choice.

What makes Lou's story powerful isn't just where she ended up, but also how she got there. She didn't rebrand herself overnight. She stayed rooted in what she did best—storytelling, human insight and strategic design—and applied it relentlessly to the context of emerging tech. Her strength wasn't in knowing the answers. It was in asking better questions.

She didn't try to 'fit in' to tech. She showed why tech needs people who think like her.

Lou's rise into AI leadership is a case study in modern career navigation. It proves that the future won't be led only by the most technical; it will be shaped by those who can translate, bridge and build with others in mind.

Lessons learned: Why Lou's story matters

Lou's rise didn't come from chasing a title but from asking better questions and being visible. She didn't position herself as the technical expert. She brought a different kind of value: curiosity, critical thinking and the ability to see around corners. While others jumped to solutions, Lou stepped back and asked, 'What problem are we actually solving?' That shift changed the conversation and her career trajectory.

She made herself visible by showing up in the right rooms, guiding strategic discussions, and helping teams connect the dots between emerging technology and real human need — clear, consistent value, delivered in the moments that mattered.

Lou's pivot is a clear reminder that you don't need to come from a tech background to shape the future of tech. She didn't step into AI leadership because she fit a typical profile. She stepped in because she brought a different lens. Her ability to think critically, design for people and lead with curiosity made her indispensable.

Lou's story is proof that deep expertise doesn't always come from the traditional places, and that people are needed at the table who think differently.

From army boots to Microsoft chief technology officer: How Sarah boldly mapped her way into the C-suite

Sarah Carney's career didn't begin in tech. It began in the military, where she had dreams of flying helicopters on peacekeeping missions. But after a serious ankle injury ended her time in service, she was forced to start over, with no plan, no backup and no idea where she'd land.

She pivoted to law, starting as a secretary in a firm and steadily carving out new roles for herself. From there, she moved into telecommunications. At every step, Sarah followed a simple, strategic pattern: choose a job she could do standing on her head, build credibility fast, and use it as a launch pad. She calls this strategy 'land and expand', and it's been the foundation of her entire career.

She joined Microsoft eight years ago, not as a technologist, but through a role in tender management. She was on maternity leave at the time, happy in her job, when a former colleague encouraged her to have a conversation. One meeting and a moment in the Microsoft foyer watching a video about the company's social impact shifted her thinking. She decided to take the position and join Microsoft.

The role she took wasn't exciting, but it gave her something more important: exposure. It put her in a position to learn the business from the inside, meet decision makers and identify where her strengths could have the most impact.

From there, she made smart, deliberate moves — not always upwards, often sideways — into roles that filled her knowledge gaps, built her network and added to her experience base. She looked at each opportunity through two lenses: 'What can I learn here?' and 'How does this get me closer to the work I actually want to be doing?'

Her focus was always the same: build the experience, fill the gaps and show up in the rooms that mattered. She invested in visibility early. She not only met the right people, but also made sure they saw her in action. She worked closely with leaders around the role she wanted long before it was available. She asked for stretch projects, joined cross-functional initiatives and made it clear to her manager what she was aiming for, as part of a long-term plan.

When the chief technology officer (CTO) role came up, she wasn't an outsider applying cold. She was already known and trusted. She didn't have to convince them she could do the job, because they'd seen her do it in pieces, consistently, over time. The formal application was a formality. She had already built the case for herself.

Sarah didn't come from a tech background, but she brought something more important. She brought clarity and structured thinking from the army, stakeholder engagement from law and strategic problem-solving from telco. And she brought a relentless focus on learning and showing up with substance.

Lessons learned: Why Sarah's story matters

Sarah's story is a masterclass in how to grow into big roles from unconventional paths — not by waiting to be chosen, but by putting yourself in position long before the opportunity arrives. Sarah's journey shows the power of pivoting and the value of knowing how to package your skills. She didn't follow a straight path.

She moved across industries, and took roles that gave her leverage. At every stage, she backed her transferable skills — from disciplined planning in the army to stakeholder management in law and telco — and learned how to frame them in ways each new industry valued. Her rise to CTO wasn't luck. It was the result of showing up in the right rooms. She didn't wait to be tapped on the shoulder; she made sure people already knew what she could do.

Sarah's story is a lesson in strategic reinvention. Careers aren't linear anymore, and the people who grow the fastest are the ones who know how to pivot with purpose, translate their strengths and position themselves for what's next.

Bold moves in action

Catie, Lou and Sarah's stories are more than just inspiration; they're evidence. They bring to life the core message of this book: that bold moves are not about waiting until you feel completely ready. They're about moving with clarity, backing your strengths and being willing to grow into the next version of yourself.

Each of these women made non-linear shifts. They pivoted across industries, stepped into unfamiliar spaces and translated their skills in new ways. They didn't have traditional backgrounds in the careers they now hold, but they made strategic choices, learned in motion and positioned themselves in rooms where decisions were being made.

They show us that confidence isn't something you have before you begin. It's something you earn by starting. They didn't wait to be chosen, and instead put themselves in the running and made sure the right people knew what they could do. They all showed resilience when things didn't go to plan and adaptability when they knew changes needed to be made.

Their stories are proof that this work matters. If you can package your value, make yourself visible and stay open to growth, what's possible is unlimited. Careers don't need to be linear. But they do need to be led with intention, with strategy and with boldness.

You are no different to these three women and if they can make bold moves and future-proof their careers so can you. The only limitations are the ones in your own mind.

Using these stories to inspire boldness in you?

Take a moment to pause and reflect. Ask yourself:

1. Which story from this chapter resonated with you the most, and why?

2. Did any part of these career journeys stir up emotions such as hope, fear, inspiration or even discomfort?

3. What does your reaction tell you about where you might be in your own career journey?

Grab a pen or open your notes app, and jot down a few thoughts. This simple reflection could be the beginning of your own bold move.

Chapter 11

The 30-Day Bold Move Challenge

O ur time together may be coming to a close, but your journey is just beginning. This is the moment of your bold move, the spark of your transformation. No more playing small. No more holding back.

This is when you step forward, unapologetically, into your next stage — confident, clear and ready for whatever comes next. This final chapter is not for reading and then putting away; it's for doing. Here is your daily bold move action plan.

Starting your 30-Day Bold Move Challenge

Confidence is a skill you can build. This 30-day challenge will empower you to future-proof your career through daily bite-sized exercises that build courage, a growth mindset, visibility, creativity and bold action-taking. Over four weeks, you'll stretch yourself in manageable ways and build momentum to pursue your ambitions with energy and conviction. Let's get started!

Week 1: Courage and mindset

In this first week, you will continue building the habit of self-belief and trust. I will ask you to be courageous and even slightly uncomfortable as you take on challenges. Each day, you'll take small steps — from affirmations to tiny acts of bravery — because confidence grows when you consistently face fears and realise that they are not red flags but signals of growth.

Day 1: Set your intentions

Begin by journalling about *why* you're committing to this challenge, what you hope to achieve and how you want to feel at the end. This is such an important step, because if you don't understand why you're embarking on this challenge, you may not be motivated to see this through.

An example of a powerful intention could be:

> *Over the next 30 days, I intend to stop playing small and start showing up as the confident, capable person I know I am. I will make decisions from a place of self-worth, not self-doubt. I am ready to step into the version of me who goes after what she wants — boldly, unapologetically and with purpose.*

You can use this intention if it resonates with you or write your own. Take your time with this exercise, because setting a clear intention and a positive tone primes your mind for confidence and growth from day one.

Day 2: Celebrate your achievements

How often do you dwell on what you haven't done or haven't achieved? One thing I know to be true is that what we focus on grows. This is your moment to shift that focus intentionally to what makes you feel proud.

Make a list of ten achievements or proud moments in your career. Big or small, every win matters. Maybe you nailed a presentation, navigated a tough conversation or picked up a new skill; if it made you feel accomplished, it counts.

Keep this 'wins list' visible. Return to it any time self-doubt creeps in. Your achievements are more than milestones; they're proof of your strength, resilience and capability.

Once you have your first ten, make sure to add to this list often. Let it serve as your personal evidence folder, reminding you that you can do hard things and you do deliver.

Day 3: Reframe a limiting belief

The thoughts you think internally dictate the actions you take externally. It's time to identify one self-doubting thought that often holds you back — for example, 'I'm not good enough to lead this project' or 'I always mess up in big meetings'. Write it down. See it for what it is — a thought, not a fact. This is the voice your inner critic that I asked you to name back in chapter 2. Remember — she no longer runs the show. She will pop up from time to time, usually when you begin to stretch yourself.

It's time to rewrite any limiting beliefs from a growth mindset perspective — for example, 'I have the skills to learn and excel at this project, even if it's a stretch'. Developing a growth mindset empowers you to cultivate self-confidence, so practise talking to yourself like a coach, not a critic.

If it helps, think about it from this framework. 'Is this the old me thinking, or is it the bold me thinking?'

Day 4: Break the pattern

Today, revisit your 'stop doing' list from chapter 3 and choose one habit to stop. Choose something that quietly chips away at your confidence or energy. Maybe it's over-apologising, doomscrolling first thing in the morning or saying 'yes' when you mean 'no'.

The goal is awareness. When you notice yourself doing the habit you want to stop, pause and choose differently. You don't have to be perfect, just intentional. One conscious interruption of a pattern can be incredibly empowering.

What will you choose to stop doing from now? Write it down, and make the commitment to yourself not to repeat this limiting pattern.

Day 5: Build the habit

Now it's time to start something that fuels your growth. Go back to your 'start doing' list from chapter 3 and pick one small, repeatable habit that supports the confident, bold version of you.

That could mean journalling one win a day, starting your mornings tech-free, going for a 30-minute walk each day or checking in with your goals before checking your inbox. Consistency builds momentum, and momentum builds confidence.

So, ask yourself: what is one bold habit you can start today that could build a better tomorrow?

Day 6: Tiny act of courage

Do one small thing outside your comfort zone today. It could be speaking up with a suggestion in a meeting, initiating a tough but necessary conversation, complimenting a colleague or manager, or even doing something solo (such as dining out alone) if that's uneasy for you.

The goal is to feel the fear and do it anyway. Often, confidence comes from realising that a fear was misplaced. You'll likely find that the outcome, even if it's not perfect, wasn't as scary as you imagined.

Day 7: Gratitude and reflection

Having a gratitude practice has changed my life in such a powerful way. I used to get to the end of the week and focus on all the things I hadn't done or achieved, which left me feeling frustrated and impatient. Over the past few years, I have made a conscious effort to flip this and instead focus on what is working, what is going well and what I am grateful for. Bringing this into my life at the end of every week has made me feel happier and more present, and dramatically changed my mindset. I hope it does the same for you.

Write down three things you're grateful for this week — for example, a supportive colleague, a skill you have, a recent breakthrough or moment of clarity. It can be a moment, an experience, a person or something you have worked on. Gratitude can boost optimism and resilience.

By appreciating your growth, you continue to build courage and set yourself up for next week with a positive, resilient mindset.

Week 2: Visibility and voice

This week focuses on stepping into the spotlight and making your voice heard. As you now know, building professional visibility is key to career growth; it pays to be seen and connected. With these challenges, you'll enhance your online presence, speak up more confidently and start sharing your expertise. Each small action will help you be recognised for the value you bring.

Day 8: Polish your profile

Let's make sure your LinkedIn profile is reflecting not the old version of you, but the bold version you're stepping into now. Today is about showing up online with intention and clarity. Your profile should reflect who you are, what you stand for and where you're headed.

Here's where to focus:

- *Headline:* Lead with where you're going, not just where you've been. Make it aspirational, clear and confident.

- *Microcredentials and recent growth:* Add any courses, skills or learning from the past year. These small details show you're evolving and serious about it.

- *About section:* This is your story, in your voice. What drives you? What do you want to be known for? Keep it human, honest and future-focused.

Update your profile like your future self is already reading it, because she is. (Head back to chapter 7 for the LinkedIn profile checklist if you're after more ideas.)

Day 9: Post on LinkedIn

Time to work on your personal brand — that's right, it's time to post on LinkedIn. Using the BOLD posting formula from chapter 7:

- **B**e seen and searchable.

- **O**wn your narrative.

- **L**ead with value.

- **D**o it consistently.

To make this nice and simple, start with sharing an interesting article with a brief note on your takeaway. Or you could share a recent microcredential you completed, or a picture of a recent event you attended with your biggest takeaway.

If posting still feels bold, remember this is about increasing visibility in a meaningful way. By adding your voice online, you signal that you're an active, knowledgeable member of your professional community, and you never know what new connection or opportunity might arise from that visibility.

Posting something for the first time is always the most challenging, but remember you are just adding value to your network, and the more value you share the more opportunities will open up to you.

Day 10: Banish 'just' and 'sorry'

For the entire day, practise communication without minimising language. Many women (myself included) use qualifiers such as 'just' and 'maybe', and use unnecessary apologies out of habit. We might preface a request with, 'Just checking in' or 'Sorry, can I ask a question?' These kinds of words can undermine your authority.

I used to do this all the time: 'Hey, just checking in' or 'Hey, sorry to bother you, I know you're busy'. I have had to work on this a lot and, to be honest, I still do. However, now that I am aware of it, I make a conscious effort to change it.

Today, catch yourself if you are about to use these qualifiers in any form of communication. State your needs and opinions confidently: 'Please provide an update', for example, or 'I have a question' or 'Circling back on this'.

You'll likely find that you sound as capable as you are, and that others respond with equal respect.

Day 11: Speak up with an idea

In your next meeting or group discussion (even a virtual one), today's challenge is to voice at least one idea or opinion. Plan ahead if you can, noting a point you could contribute or a question you could ask. If meetings aren't on your schedule today, you could share an idea with your team via email or a work chat.

The goal here is to break the pattern of staying silent. Many women hesitate to reach for the next step, not because they lack ability, but because they've been conditioned to wait for permission.

This is your practice ground for backing yourself. Every time you speak up, you're sharing your voice, and you're reminding yourself and everyone else that your perspective matters.

Day 12: Reach out and reconnect

Networking time. Today, reach out to someone in your professional network. This could be a former manager, an ex-colleague in your industry or someone you recently met at an event.

Send a short message to check in or compliment them on a recent achievement. If appropriate, suggest a coffee chat or ask a question about their current projects.

Most opportunities don't come from job boards; they come from people, and often people you are already connected to. According to LinkedIn's 2024 *Global Talent Trends* report, up to 85 per cent of critical roles are filled through networking. When you build real relationships, you're not just opening doors, but also creating them.

Strengthening your network now is a bold move. It's a direct investment in your future opportunities and a powerful way to build confidence through conversation, connection and visibility. (Review chapter 7 for more tips on networking online and in person.)

Day 13: Perfect your pitch

Practise a one-minute 'elevator pitch' about yourself. Imagine you meet a senior leader or someone new at a networking event. One of their first questions is, 'What do you do?' or 'Can you tell me about yourself?'

Write down a concise, compelling answer. Focus on where you want to go and highlight growing skills; this will set you apart. For example:

I'm a [name current role] *with a growing focus on AI. I've been deepening my skills through hands-on projects and targeted learning, and I'm excited to step into roles that blend technology, strategy and real-world impact.*

Practise saying this response out loud and confidently. I like to record myself on my phone. You could even use the voice function in ChatGPT and ask for feedback.

This exercise is about feeling prepared and refining your voice, so that next time you need to introduce yourself, you can immediately showcase the value you bring.

Day 14: Own your achievements

Today, share a recent win or achievement with someone else. It could be in a team meeting, during a one-on-one with your manager, or even via a LinkedIn post celebrating a project completion or lesson learned.

If self-promotion feels uncomfortable, frame it as sharing gratitude or insights ('I'm proud our team accomplished x; it taught me y'). The key is not to keep your accomplishments hidden. Women often hesitate to spotlight their success, but visibility is crucial for career advancement.

By acknowledging something you did well, you reinforce your self-worth and let your network know what you can do. No shrinking back! Give yourself credit, because you've earned it.

Week 3: Skill building and creativity

In a fast-changing world, continuous learning is not a luxury but a necessity for future-proofing your career. As I outline in chapter 5, curiosity and lifelong learning are among the top five human skills that will be in demand over the next ten years (and beyond).

This week, it's time to stretch your skill set and creative muscles. Trying new tools and creative exercises will not only expand your capabilities but also energise you. Plus, learning new things is a great confidence booster.

Remember — creativity and innovation are foundational skills in many businesses, and cultivating them will set you apart. It's time to embrace a beginner's mindset and have fun with these challenges.

Day 15: Identify a future skill

Revisit chapter 5 on the future-fit skills that will propel your career forward and are the most in demand over the coming decade. Pick one 'hard' skill that you want to work on and feel will be the most beneficial in your current role or future role.

Write down the skill you want to learn, *why* it's important and one small step to begin. For example:

- *Skill:* 'Become AI literate.'

- *Why:* 'Because I know this is the number one skill companies are asking for right now, and I want to ensure I am staying ahead and future-proofing my career.'

- *One small step:* Sign up for a free online intro course and work towards getting that microcredential, or visit Pivotr.com and start a seven-day learning sprint.

Proactively acquiring new skills keeps you adaptable and valuable; upskilling is now essential to career growth. Today's challenge is the first step to making learning a habit.

Day 16: Try a new AI tool

Let today be a play day. Spend 20 to 30 minutes exploring a new AI tool — perhaps something you've never used before, or one you've been curious about but haven't made time for.

At the time of writing, you already have hundreds of tools to choose from, including Microsoft Copilot, Google Gemini, ChatGPT, Lovable, Jasper, Claude or Replit. The list keeps growing and more options will no doubt be available by the time this book is published. The key isn't to master them all but to stay open, stay curious and don't be afraid to try.

You could:

- ask an AI tool for help brainstorming ideas or outlining a task you've been avoiding

- use a voice-to-text tool to quickly capture your thoughts

- play with a design or writing tool to reimagine your LinkedIn bio, create some great content or summarise a news article for you

- test an automation that could save you time in your workflow.

Your results don't have to be perfect or even particularly useful at first. The goal is to build your comfort with experimenting. Every time you try a new tool, you're training your mind to adapt, learn and lead in a tech-driven world.

That's the muscle you're building here, and remember — courage comes before confidence.

Day 17: Ten ideas brainstorm

Today, you will focus on building a human skill and strengthening your creativity and problem-solving capabilities. (Review chapter 5 for more on the required human skills for the next decade.)

Choose a work or personal challenge and brainstorm ten ideas or solutions in one sitting. For instance, 'Ten ideas to improve team meetings', or 'Ten side-business ideas for my passion', or 'Ten ways to use AI in my current role', or 'Ten content ideas to build my personal brand'.

Aim for quantity over quality and write down as many ideas as you can. If you think of more than ten, that's great; keep going, don't limit your thinking.

Even if only one or two ideas are viable, you've exercised your creative brain. This technique builds mental flexibility and reminds you that you're an innovative thinker.

The more often you do this, the easier idea-generation gets. Creativity is a skill that is built the more you use it.

Day 18: Learn from an expert (microlearning)

Carve out a short time block (20 to 30 minutes) to learn something new or improve a skill you have identified as a knowledge gap. You could watch a TED Talk or webinar on a topic you find interesting, listen to a podcast interview with a leader in your field or read a how-to article on a new skill.

Pick something outside your usual niche to broaden your perspective. This could be a talk on creative thinking or emotional intelligence, or an article on how to lead through change and uncertainty.

This quick infusion of knowledge not only adds to your skill toolkit but also keeps you in a growth mindset. When you see the world as full of things to learn, you stay adaptable and confident when facing new challenges.

Day 19: Apply your new skill

Take one thing you've learned recently, perhaps from the challenges from days 16 to 18, and put it into practice in a small way.

If you are beginning to work on your AI skills, apply them today. You could ask ChatGPT to help you prepare for an upcoming presentation or meeting, for example. You could use Jasper to come up with some new marketing copy to help with conversion rates. You could use Google Sheets plus Gemini to quickly summarise data or spot trends with AI-generated charts. You could even try Replit and spin up a website. (Seriously — give it a go!) The possibilities are endless, so put your new AI skills into practice.

The point is to bridge knowledge into action. Using a skill in context solidifies your learning and boosts confidence as you prove to yourself you can integrate new skills into your work. It's okay if it initially feels clumsy; you're gaining momentum as a lifelong learner.

Day 20: Do something creative for fun

Reignite your creative energy by doing a fun creative activity unrelated to your day job. Spend at least 30 minutes on a creative hobby or a new craft — start a blog, for example, sketch or paint, play an instrument, write a short story of a recent bold move you made, cook a new recipe or try a DIY project.

The purpose of this challenge is to engage the right side of your brain and enjoy the process of making something. Creativity isn't just for artists; it improves problem-solving and can reduce stress. When I return to work after a weekend of doing something creative, I find I am often more inspired and resourceful.

Plus, a creative activity proves that you can learn and create in any arena, which builds the mindset that you can handle new challenges at work creatively too.

Day 21: Share and reflect on growth

You've been building skills and creativity all week. Take a moment to feel proud. By showing up for yourself in this way, you build trust and prove that you are someone who does what she sets out to achieve. That's the kind of momentum that leads to the boldest of moves.

Once you have reflected on the new skills you have learned, share them with a close friend, your community or a loved one.

Remember — this isn't about bragging, but is about celebrating the moment while sharing lessons. This is a powerful way to encourage others you care about to begin thinking about how they could also be future-proofing their careers. That's how we start a 'bold move' movement!

Also, consider sharing one insight or tip from this week on LinkedIn. Publicly sharing learnings and lessons boosts your visibility as a curious, growth-minded professional and reinforces what you've gained.

Be sure to continue this growth mindset, because it will serve you well as you move into planning bigger moves next week.

Week 4: Bold career moves and planning

In the final stretch of your 30-day challenge, you'll channel your confidence into concrete career moves and strategic planning. This week is about thinking big and taking action: envisioning your future, making bold asks and setting plans to reach your goals.

You are more qualified than you give yourself credit for. You don't need to wait on permission or the 'perfect timing'. This week, you'll map out your aspirations and start turning them into reality, one bold step at a time.

Day 22: Envision your future

Find a quiet moment to imagine your career five years from now. Consider the following:

- What does your ideal role look like?

- What kind of work are you doing, and what impact are you making?

- What would success look like to you?

- What does your perfect day look like?

- Where are you living?

- What values are firmly in place?

- What type of company are you working for?

Go deep. Really take a moment to write a descriptive 'vision statement' or draw a mind map of your future career scenario. Be bold and aspirational; don't limit yourself by current fears.

This exercise clarifies *what* you're aiming for, and planning a journey is easier when you know the destination. Today is not about setting a goal; that will come. Today is simply thinking about what's important to you and where you see yourself in the future. The more you seek clarity today, the easier it will be when you begin taking the next steps to achieve it.

Enjoy this exercise and don't hold yourself back.

Day 23: Who do you need to become?

You've got clear on what you want. Now it's time to step into who you need to become to make your vision real, because big goals require a bigger version of you — not louder or busier, but bolder.

Think of her now, the future you who already has the thing you want. Ask yourself:

- How does she show up? Start describing her in detail.

- Does she walk with certainty and presence?

- Does she take up space with her voice, her ideas and her energy?

- Does she speak clearly and with intention?

- Does she know her worth?

- Does she make decisions from her vision, rather than from fear?

The bigger, bolder version of you isn't perfect, but she's practising confidence, courage and consistency.

Once you have written out and gotten clear on who you need to become in this next bold chapter, your job is to start being her, right now.

Ask yourself:

- What's one habit or belief you need to *stop* to become her?

- What's one small way you can *start* acting like her today, before you 'feel ready'?

- What would she do next?

From my experience in setting goals, it's never about the end destination. The real transformation is who you become along the way. That starts now.

Day 24: Set a bold (but doable) career goal

Let's take your vision and turn it into a bold step forward. This step shouldn't be something overwhelming, but needs to be something intentional that stretches you just enough. Choose one bold-but-achievable career goal, something just outside your current comfort zone but 100 per cent within reach if you back yourself.

Here are some examples:

- sign up for a professional event or networking meet-up

- gain a microcredential and share it on LinkedIn

- reach out to someone in your dream role and ask for a 15-minute chat

- start writing a post that shares your career journey or learnings

- put your hand up for a stretch project at work

- pitch yourself for a podcast, panel or guest article

- refresh your résumé and apply for a role that excites you, even if you're not 'fully ready'.

What's your goal? Why does it matter to you? Write it down.

Naming your goal makes it real, and sharing it with a friend, your community, mentor or even publicly can help lock in accountability. This isn't about putting a tonne of pressure on yourself; it's about gaining momentum. It's about making progress, rather than aiming for perfection.

Today, you commit to the next version of you.

Day 25: Update your résumé or portfolio

Take some time today to refresh your résumé and, if you have one, a personal website or portfolio. Add in recent achievements from the past year, update your summary to align with the bold goal you set, and ensure your key skills are highlighted.

Often we don't update these profiles until we need to, but proactively maintaining them is empowering. The process reminds you of how much you've accomplished and can be an instant confidence boost. It also prepares you to seize unexpected opportunities. I recently had a role I was headhunting for, and the woman I reached out to wasn't actively looking. However, she said to me, 'I always keep my résumé updated, just in case an exciting opportunity presented itself'. Her CV was great, and I could introduce her skills to the client that day. She wasn't scrambling to throw something together. She was quietly and confidently prepared for her next bold move.

Today's challenge is packaging your value so you're ready to shine when a big chance comes. Dust down your CV and make sure it is up to date with all your skills, experience and qualifications. Every time you learn something new, get into the habit of adding it straight to your résumé, so when an opportunity comes (which it will when you begin to be more visible online), you are ready to move.

Day 26: Build your personal board of advisers

Imagine for a moment you are sitting in a boardroom with five empty seats. You have a bold idea or are ready to make your next bold move. Now consider:

- Who do you want to be sitting beside you in your boardroom, helping you make these decisions?

- Who do you want guiding, coaching or mentoring you?

- Who has achieved great things and is where you would like to be in five years?

- Who supports you and cheers you on?

- Who challenges you in a good way?

- Who keeps you calm in uncertainty?

Your board of advisers can be anyone; they don't need to be people you know personally. They can be people you admire, business gurus whose content you consume, or close family and friends you trust.

In my boardroom, I like to have a mix of people. Some I have never met, but I consume their content. I listen to their podcasts, watch their YouTube videos, subscribe to their blogs, buy their courses and read their books. Others are close friends and family members who I know have my back. And others are a few steps ahead of where I want to be.

Now it's time to write down your five-person board of directors. These five individuals are your sounding boards. Make sure you include a few people who you can call and have access to, and maybe one or two whom you follow and can learn from. The key here is that you need people around you who want the best for you, but who also open your mind, challenge your thinking, and provide energy.

They say you are the average of the five people you spend the most time with, which is why you want to be selective about who you get advice from and who you surround yourself with the most. Your board doesn't have to be formal, and it doesn't have to be forever. But it does have to reflect the direction you're heading, not just where you've been.

And as you grow, evolve, and take bigger and bolder moves, don't be afraid to upgrade your board. Build your circle with intention, because who you're becoming deserves to be surrounded by people who see it, even before you fully do.

Day 27: Ask for what you want

Think of one thing you want to advocate for in your current role. This could be a raise, a promotion, or a new responsibility or project that would help you grow. You could also ask for more flexibility, if you feel that would help you show up better at home and in the office.

Today, outline your case for whatever you're asking for. Write down your accomplishments, how you've added value and why you're ready for this. Stick to the facts, not the emotion. In chapter 8, I cover negotiation strategies in detail, and now it's time to put that into practice.

If possible, discuss your request with your manager or HR, or schedule a meeting for later this month.

If you're not in a position to ask for something at work right now, practise a negotiation scenario in other areas of your life. Set boundaries around your time or energy, such as not answering texts after a certain time. Ask for more help around the house or for more shared responsibility, so you can free up time to work on what matters to you.

Women often hesitate to negotiate or wait to be given things; today, you break that pattern.

You may not get the answer you want, and that's okay. The more you practise, the more you'll see no as a stepping stone to success, and that builds resilience and agility — two skills that are necessary for the future of work.

This isn't about making demands; it's about advocating for yourself, which takes courage. By now, you know where that leads!

Day 28: Take a bold leap

On day 24, you set a bold but doable career goal — something slightly out of your comfort zone but 100 per cent within reach if you backed yourself.

Now it's time to keep taking action, and keep the wheels in motion. Pick one real, visible step that moves you toward that goal today. For example:

- If you said you'd attend a networking even, sign up for one now.

- If you wanted to build your visibility, draft that LinkedIn post or pitch yourself for a panel.

- If you're working toward a pivot, reach out to someone in your dream field.

- If you're aiming for a job change, submit an application, even if you're not 'fully ready'.

Your leap doesn't need to be perfect, but it does need to be real.

The truth is most people stay stuck not because they don't know what they want, but because they wait to feel ready. You're not waiting anymore.

Even if you're nervous, do the thing. That is confidence in motion. That's what creates change. Today, you stop circling the edge and step into the next version of you.

Day 29: Write a letter from future you

Today, you're going to tap into one of the most powerful confidence tools out there: vision-backed self-belief.

Write a letter from the woman you are one year from now, the woman who committed to her bold goal and followed through. Speak to yourself like a mentor or coach, cheering you on from the other side of transformation.

Picture yourself standing at the edge of that shaky bridge, the one I talk about in chapter 3 that stretches across the bold gap. On the other side, you see her: the future version of you. She locks eyes with you and calls out, 'Keep going. I know it's scary now, but everything you're walking through is shaping who I've become. And I promise — it's worth it'.

When writing the letter, use these prompts to guide you:

- Where are you now?

- What does life look like a year from now in your career, confidence, energy and focus?

- What have you achieved?

- What habits or beliefs did you let go of?

- What bold moves made the biggest difference?

- What do you want to say to the 'you' reading this today?

- Who have you become?

Let this letter be something you come back to. A reminder of what's possible when you trust yourself. Keep it in your journal, tuck it into your laptop case or record it as a voice note.

The bold version of you is not far away. She's already unfolding, one move at a time.

Day 30: Celebrate and plan your next chapter

You made it to day 30 — congratulations! Take some time today to celebrate your progress. Look back at your journal entries and notes. Notice how far you've come in just a month — including mindset shifts, actions taken, fears overcome and new habits formed.

Treat yourself to something enjoyable, such as an outing, a favourite meal or time with someone who supports you as a reward. Pause long enough to savour this moment and what you have achieved or what you have begun. Celebrating the milestone moments is so important because it builds momentum, and that's what continues to build confidence.

Finally, plan forward: write down three concrete actions you will commit to in the next three months to continue this growth. These actions might be extensions of things you have already started — for example, 'attend one networking event each month', 'apply for a leadership program' or 'continue weekly LinkedIn posts'.

Seal your plan with a simple promise to yourself: you will keep choosing courage and growth even after this challenge stops, and you finish this book.

You could even set yourself another 30-day challenge. You could choose one of the in-demand skills discussed in chapter 5, for example, and commit to it for the next month. The point is to not stop making bold moves and backing yourself. You've proven you can push past comfort and invest in yourself. With your confidence boosted and a bold plan in hand, you're ready to stride into your next bold move and the future you envision, on your terms!

CONCLUSION
YOU'RE READY NOW

At the beginning of this book, I had one intention: to show you that the boldest moves don't start with certainty. They start with a decision — a decision to back yourself and to begin, before you feel ready.

One of the biggest myths about confidence is that it comes first, and you have to feel it before you take action. But if you wait for the confidence to come, you'll wait forever. And that bold move you're dreaming of might never happen.

This is what I want you to understand now more than ever. The future belongs to those who are brave enough to say, 'I don't know how to do that yet, but I know I can figure it out'.

You've seen this firsthand from all the stories of career pivots and transitions throughout this book. None of these women, including me, felt ready to change careers, step up into leadership or start their own thing. They all felt fear and impostor syndrome and doubted whether they had what it took to succeed. But instead of focusing on the worst-case scenario or worrying about what others would think, they made themselves a priority, got clear on why it was important and took action.

The truth is you don't need to have your whole path mapped out. You just need to take the next bold step. When you do this, you back yourself and build trust in your abilities to figure things out. At the same time, you show others what's possible and, in the process, create a ripple effect around you. When one woman rises, we all rise. I acknowledge it's difficult to be what you can't see, but let's turn that on its head. If you can't see it, be it. Be the woman who backs herself unapologetically, who advocates for what she wants and takes charge of her life and career.

As the world of work continues to evolve with AI, automation and new ways of working, you'll need more than a polished résumé. You'll need adaptability, curiosity and the confidence to speak up, learn in real-time and show up even when the rules are still being written.

The good news is that you've already started building those future-fit skills. Every bold move you've made throughout this book — whether it was reaching out to someone, updating your LinkedIn or having a courageous conversation — has prepared you for what's next.

Now, pause for a moment and imagine her: the version of you one year from now, the woman who kept saying yes to herself. Imagine that woman who stepped forward, not back, who launched the idea, pivoted into AI, had the conversation and took the risk.

She's not a stranger; she's you just a few bold moves ahead. How can you practise being bold today, not someday?

Decide. Begin. Become.

You're not just ready for what's next. You are the kind of woman who shapes the future around her, one bold move at a time.

With confidence
Georgie x

ACKNOWLEDGEMENTS

To my husband, Kyle, thank you for being my biggest cheerleader, my sounding-board and my steady anchor, not only through every draft, doubt, and deadline of this book, but also through life itself. Your support has made dreams possible.

To my family.

Mum, thank you for showing me what self-belief and confidence look like in real-time. I never saw or heard you put yourself down and, as a young woman, that gave me some solid foundations to walk on. Every day, your example echoes in how I show up and carry myself.

Dad, thank you for showing me what it takes to succeed. Your work ethic and drive inspired me and showed me what resilience looks like in action. I carry those lessons with me every single day.

My brother, thank you for being the only person who can make me laugh so hard that I cry. Never lose that; it's a gift the world needs. You are proof that you can turn your passion into a career, which has inspired me more than you know.

To my extended family, I may not see you as often as I would like, but you all helped shape who I am today. Thank you for giving me the confidence, resilience and independence to chase dreams that once felt too big to say aloud. I love you all, and you've been the roots that keep me grounded and growing.

To my best friend and business partner, Pam, thank you for your unwavering support and unmatched sense of humour, and for the lightness you bring to even the craziest of days. Building a business with you hasn't just been possible; it's also been a joy. There's truly no-one else I'd rather be on this wild, wonderful ride with.

To my incredible friends, your daily inspiration, encouragement and fierce loyalty remind me of what's possible when women support women.

And to you, the reader who has put your trust in me, who showed up with curiosity and courage, thank you. I wrote this book for you. I hope it meets you right where you are and helps you take your next bold move.

NEXT STEPS

Free AI courses

To help you stay relevant in the age of AI, I've pulled together a curated list of free online courses that cover the fundamentals of artificial intelligence (AI), along with aspects such as prompt engineering, ethical use and practical tools for everyday work. Whether you're new to AI or looking to sharpen your skills, these courses are a great starting point to build your confidence and stay ahead in a rapidly evolving career landscape.

Just go to www.georgiehubbard.com/ai-courses to get started.

AI-powered career mentor

To support you beyond the pages of this book, I've founded Pivotr, an AI-powered career tool designed to help you keep making bold moves with clarity and confidence. Whether you want to step up into leadership, shift into a new industry or start something of your own, Pivotr gives you a personalised roadmap, helps you set intentional goals and turns your next chapter into an actionable plan.

Visit pivotr.com to begin your journey toward the future and the career you deserve.

LET'S CONNECT

I'd love to stay in touch and continue supporting you as you make your next bold move.

Follow me and join the conversation here:

- **LinkedIn:** www.linkedin.com/in/georgiehubbard/

- **Instagram:** @georgielhubbard

- **TikTok:** @georgie_hubbard

- **X (formerly Twitter):** x.com/georgielhubbard

- **Podcast:** *Career Confidence* — available on Spotify, Apple Podcasts and all major platforms

- **Website:** www.georgiehubbard.com

I would love to hear what resonated with you from the book, what you're taking action on, your next bold move or just to say hello.